hungry authors

hungry authors

The Indispensable Guide to Planning, Writing, and Publishing a Nonfiction Book

LIZ MORROW
ARIEL CURRY
Foreword by Allison Fallon

Rowman & Littlefield
Lanham • Boulder • New York • London

Published by Rowman & Littlefield
An imprint of The Rowman & Littlefield Publishing Group, Inc.
4501 Forbes Boulevard, Suite 200, Lanham, Maryland 20706
www.rowman.com

86-90 Paul Street, London EC2A 4NE, United Kingdom

British Library Cataloguing in Publication Information Available

Library of Congress Cataloging-in-Publication Data

Names: Morrow, Liz, 1986– author. ǀ Curry, Ariel, 1989– author. ǀ Fallon,
    Allison, writer of foreword.
Title: Hungry authors : the indispensable guide to planning, writing, and
    publishing a nonfiction book / Liz Morrow, Ariel Curry ; foreword by
    Allison Fallon.
Description: Lanham : Rowman & Littlefield, 2024. ǀ Includes
    bibliographical references and index. ǀ Summary: "In Hungry Authors,
    industry insiders Liz Murrow and Ariel Curry teach aspiring nonfiction
    authors with important messages and great ideas how to envision,
    write, plan, pitch, and publish an amazing book"— Provided by
    publisher.
Identifiers: LCCN 2023056455 (print) ǀ LCCN 2023056456 (ebook) ǀ ISBN
    9781538187326 (paperback) ǀ ISBN 9781538187333 (epub)
Subjects: LCSH: Authorship—Vocational guidance. ǀ Authorship—
    Handbooks, manuals, etc. ǀ Prose literature—Technique.
Classification: LCC PN151 .M74 2024 (print) ǀ LCC PN151 (ebook) ǀ
    DDC 808.02--dc23/eng/20240525
LC record available at https://lccn.loc.gov/2023056455
LC ebook record available at https://lccn.loc.gov/2023056456

For authors everywhere who are hungry for it.
We believe in you.

Contents

*Hungry Author [*huhng-gree aw-ther*]
Noun

1. A writer who is determined to succeed. They want to and will be published. They take feedback well and don't shy away from the hard work. You will find their butts in the chairs and fingers on the keyboard. They believe in their ideas and know they will impact others.

See also: persistent creator, dogged scribe, resolute wordsmith, serious word-slinger, decided originator, steadfast producer, tenacious composer, one who does not mess around

See also: You.

Authors' Note

Though we did our best, we couldn't include every single thing we know about how to write a nonfiction book in these pages. So we compiled all of our additional resources on the website hungryauthors.com/book. If you want to dig even deeper into this process, there you will find additional resources, templates, examples, trainings, and a writing community waiting to welcome you with open arms.

Foreword

by Allison Fallon, best-selling author of
The Power of Writing It Down and
Write Your Story

The large majority of those who hope to write a book will never actually do it. I know, I wish I could start with something more uplifting, but it's important for you to know. Each year thousands of people *start* writing their books and somewhere along the line they lose momentum. They hesitate. They tell themselves that they aren't "real" writers, that somebody else has already written the book they want to write, and that nobody will read it anyway.

They give up.

I know this, in part, because this is what the statistics share. Depending on the source, data suggests somewhere between 90 to 95 percent of hopeful authors will never actualize their books. Aside from the data, though, I've spent the last decade and a half of my life helping these exact wavering writers overcome familiar blocks.

As a book coach and ghostwriter, my job is to help an author find the thread of what's most interesting about their story or idea and to take that thread to turn it into a cohesive book idea. In my work, I meet an endless stream of brilliant thinkers who have something compelling to say and yet I spend *most* of my time reassuring them that their unique experience, their angle on a topic, is worth the space it will take up on the bookshelf.

You'd be shocked at how reliably imposter syndrome shows up when someone tries to write a book.

Or maybe you aren't shocked. Maybe you *are* that wavering writer. Maybe you're like Kate, my client who is a savvy and accomplished businesswoman, an actress, a mother of four, an absolutely vibrant and fascinating conversationalist who *still* questioned whether writing a book was something she could achieve. Her friends and colleagues, of course. But her? She second-guessed her writing ability, her grammar fluency, and her ability to stay on task for the months it would take to complete.

She wasn't even sure what exactly she would write about. She had ideas, sure, but couldn't seem to identify one *central* idea that felt like "The Idea," and she worried there wasn't anything substantial enough to justify an entire book.

And by the way, it wasn't like Kate needed something else on her plate. She was the founder of a multimillion-dollar empire and a dedicated mother. She was an involved community member and on the board at her children's school. She mentored young women and had what was sometimes a grueling travel schedule. The last thing she needed was something else on her to-do list.

Maybe like Kate, you understand the feeling of being brilliant at *your* thing, but at *this* thing—writing a book? Writing a book feels different.

On the surface, writing a book feels different because it is an enormous task with a massive learning curve. I've written fourteen books in my career and even I feel overwhelmed, at times, at the enormity of the book-writing task. From a blank page to a finished book can be intimidating even for a seasoned writer. That doesn't even take into account the work of getting the book into the hands of readers.

But you need to know that on top of that, writing a book feels different because you've been trained to believe by a lifetime of conditioning that writing is for "some" people but not for everyone. Not for *you*, that's for sure. Book-writing is for "those people" who have fancy degrees from famous universities, who have a certain way of saying a thing that makes it particularly poetic, or who hold a set of privileges that allow them access to the sacred space of publishing.

We've been taught to believe that some ideas are worthy of being memorialized but not *our* ideas. Not *my* idea. But where is the dividing line between the ideas that deserve to be published and those that do not? When you try to find it, it moves or even vanishes altogether. Like a shadow that shifts with the time of day, it ebbs and flows and sometimes even disappears.

Does it even exist?

Kate did eventually publish her book and to nobody's surprise but hers, it performed well in the marketplace and is currently having an impact on hundreds of thousands of readers. But before we get stuck on that outcome—which is no doubt an incredible accomplishment—I want to emphasize that before Kate's book landed in the hand of a single reader, it did something else. It changed Kate herself.

Here is a woman who had always been brilliant and creative but didn't always see what exactly made her life and perspective so valuable. In writing her book, she found what we call in publishing the One Golden Thread. She uncovered the question her life was asking and began to see the answer. She found that particular brand of brilliance that is hers and only hers. She opted herself into a world where her life and unique take were just as interesting as the writers she idolized and admired.

Nobody did that for her. She did it for herself. She did it by writing her book.

Let me ask you a question: even if Kate had never shared her book with anyone, would the outcome of finding her own voice have been worth it? She might not have been on a billboard in Times Square but she would have carried herself differently, seen herself accurately, been in tune with the weight and substance she actually carried.

Which one feels more "worth it" to you?

Writing your book may or may not get you a traditional publishing deal (although I really hope it does if that's what you're looking for). It may or may not get you a spot on the *New York Times* list. It may or may not earn you a billboard in Times Square. With this book in your hands, each of those outcomes are more attainable than they would be otherwise, but there are no guarantees except for one: I can *guarantee* you that writing your book will give you more of yourself. It will show you what makes you so interesting. It will change the way you hold yourself, the way you carry yourself through the world.

Writing your book will give you the gift of *you*, which in turn you get to share with others. And yet in order to get any of that, you will have to actually write the darn thing.

What I've found is that the authors who start *and* finish writing their books have a few things in common.

First, they welcome the idea that *wanting* to write a book is enough of a reason to do it. Most aspiring authors are looking for what they would call a "more compelling" reason. By that they mean something like a book deal or an agent or publisher knocking on their door. They want someone *else* to want them to write their book, in addition to them, because their own wanting to do it feels narcissistic, or maybe even borderline delusional.

Recently I was working with a client—I'll call him Jack—who was struggling with this concept. He was working on a business book that had a unique spiritual twist. I found him to be fascinating and his life seemed to be queuing up stories for him to share such a *different* take on a business book. At one point in our day together he turned to me.

"Who am I to write this book?" He asked.

I thought about it for a minute and then opened my mouth to speak and something unexpected came out. "You're nobody," I said.

In other words, it doesn't matter who you are or aren't. Don't get stuck on that. Those qualifiers are useless. If it's narcissistic to write a book, then it's also narcissistic to do much of anything—start a family, run a business, knit a scarf. We do these things for both practical reasons and creative ones. Because this is what it means to be a human being, to make meaning out of our existence.

Why should publishing be any different?

To write a book is not to center yourself in the middle of the human conversation. It's to center yourself in the middle of *one* conversation. The conversation about you and your life and what really matters. You want to do this because it is human instinct to do this. It is in your nature. Let that reason be enough.

Authors who finish their books also hold loosely to when or how the book will be published. Of course it's wonderful to inform yourself and know your publishing options. It can also be additive to have an intention or a publishing path in mind. *Hungry Authors* is going to help you do exactly that. But I find authors who are dead-set on publishing in a certain way or at a certain time might finish *a* book but it's not usually *the* book they were trying to write.

Sometimes writing the "wrong" book can feel as frustrating as never writing your book in the first place.

You have infinite publishing possibilities in front of you. Some of the publishing possibilities for your book may not even exist yet as you are reading these words. Like the rest of the world, publishing is changing at lightning speed and you have *no idea* what could be possible for you once you get your manuscript written. What a beautiful and compelling time to be an aspiring author!

For now, see if you can focus on trusting yourself enough to write the book that is trying to be written through you. Let the publishing details work themselves out.

What is the one idea that you want to leave with humanity forever? What is the one story that you are dying to share? What is the one question your life is asking that you must answer come hell or high water? What is so compelling about you and your idea that no reader could possibly turn away? Writing a book is as much about uncovering the answers to those questions as it is about sharing the answer with others.

Write your book to you, first.

As for me, I don't think you're a statistic. I think you're hungry. You're holding this book, after all, and something that remains inexplicable to you seems to be pulling you to take on this task. You have something to say that you don't even fully understand just yet—but you will if and when you get the thing on paper. You deserve that. Give that gift to yourself.

Moving your idea from your brain to paper can feel intimidating, yes. But it will also feel incredibly cathartic and relieving. It's an amazing way to connect with yourself, and in turn, with others. It has a way of showing you to yourself for the first time. You've been stuck in the weeds wondering if you had what it took to get to the finish line but now, finally, you have two brilliant and qualified guides to get you there.

I can't wait to see what you write.

Introduction

Welcome to the Club

Here's the truth, plain and simple: Any author with a great idea, a boatload of gumption, and a plan can write and publish a kick-ass nonfiction book. It's one of the bravest, most daring things to do—to put your heart and soul on the line for the chance of making the world a better place. Not everyone has the guts to do it. But you do—that's why you're here. Welcome to the club!

With all of the incredible, fresh voices and publishing options out there, there is no reason why writers with a message or a story can't share it with an outstanding book. Sometimes, the publishing world can feel like a mysterious clique that many people want to belong to but few actually do, usually because they don't know how to get in. But the good news is, you don't need permission! You just need some guidance and grit. There's no secret password or handshake barring you from this group. We're here to throw open the doors to this clubhouse and welcome you with open arms.

If this book is in your hand/Kindle, you're probably a lot like a former client of mine (Liz's). Brittany Estes first came to me because, like all of Ariel's and my clients, she knew she had a book in her. She is a speaker and life coach, and had a message she deeply believed people needed to hear. She hired me to work on her book proposal. I had been ghostwriting and working on book proposals for a few years and a couple of things about this project stood out to me immediately. The first was that Brittany did not have much of a platform. She had less than two thousand Instagram followers and a couple of hundred email subscribers. That was it. I knew this would be an obstacle for her in traditional publishing. I told her exactly that, but she didn't seem deterred. That was the second thing that stood out to me. Brittany was tenacious. She was the kind of client who I knew was going to do everything I suggested and not stop pitching agents and reworking the proposal until she achieved her goals. She was hungry for it. That is the exact kind of client I love to work with.

Despite her grit, though, there were things that needed improvement. Her platform, of course, wasn't a strength, but her idea and her writing also needed sharpening. Brittany was an outstanding student and within a few months, we had a proposal she was proud of and one that I knew she could sell if she just found the right agent. We drew up a query letter and Brittany began pitching. To be completely honest, I was a little nervous. I knew Brittany had the gumption to keep going and I knew her idea was fantastic and marketable, as we'd spent the last few months refining it. But you never know. Sometimes, for one reason or another, things just don't work out the way you hope they will. I didn't want Brittany to get disappointed if the process took a long time (it usually does) or if an agent gave hard-to-take feedback (they often do).

She did receive at least ten rejections, but all it took was one yes. Within a few months, Brittany landed an outstanding agent at a reputable agency and a few months after that she had her first book deal. That book did well enough that she secured another deal and today she's working on her second book with the same publisher.

After working with Brittany, something clicked for me, something I'd had a hunch was true but hadn't proven. Until then, I'd mostly worked with entrepreneurs and thought leaders who had decent platforms to begin with. Assuming they had a strong idea and some marketing chops, I was always confident we could sell their book. But after I worked with Brittany, I realized that this process—the exact one we'll teach you in this book—works for everyone, with or without a platform. And this doesn't just apply to those wanting a traditional book deal. You may want to hybrid or self-publish (which can be great options and we'll teach you how and why to pursue them). Regardless, this information will help you achieve your publishing dreams no matter what path you take.

Almost all aspiring authors we talk to feel like Brittany did. Tell us if any of these resonate.

- **You feel like you have a book inside of you.** Maybe it's still just a small voice whispering in the quiet, or perhaps it's been there long enough that it's practically screaming at you all day long. Either way, it's becoming hard to ignore.
- **You have a message you want to get out into the world.** You know something useful that you want to share to help others. You have an incredible story that will be an inspiration. You teach something that you want to codify for posterity. You believe something you want to convince others of. You've been through a transformation and you're going to walk people through it. You have a legacy you want to leave behind. Whatever it is, don't be bashful. You have a message to share.
- **You want to write a book that sells.** Passion projects exist, and they can be a worthwhile venture, but most people who come to us want their books to sell. And why wouldn't they? Books are a tremendous effort and they're meant to be shared, and that means people need to want to buy them. Not that it's the point here, but authors (you) also deserve to be paid for them.

- **You want to write a book you're proud of.** Not much feels better than a job well done. Not only do you want to spread your message by people buying your book, but you want to be proud of what's inside it. This is usually the point where people turn to us. They realize that writing a book without guidance is tough.
- **You want to write a book that makes an impact on the world.** This is the ultimate goal, isn't it? To write something that changes people and outlives you. This is at the heart of every author's reason for writing. Hell, it's our reason for writing, too. There isn't a goal nobler than wanting to change the world and make a difference, even if it's just in your own small way.

But the truth is, most people don't end up writing a book. After working with hundreds of clients, we've collated a list of reasons why this is. Let's bullet point again, shall we?

- **They don't know how.** Simple enough, right? Most people haven't written a book, so they don't yet know how. Because most people can read and write, they often *think* they can write a book. But it doesn't take long before they realize it's much more difficult than they assumed.
- **They don't know if their idea is good.** We hear this All. The. Time. I had a multimillionaire celebrity client who retired at forty-five and is best friends with a Kardashian ask me recently if their "idea is any good." Not that being a celebrity inherently allows you good ideas, but my point is: *everyone* worries that their story isn't interesting. You have a good idea in you. You have an interesting story to tell. We'll show you how.
- **They don't have a big platform.** This can be an obstacle to traditional publishing. It can also be a hindrance in getting the word out about your book. But like what happened with Brittany, it's possible to publish a great

book with a small platform. We'll make the argument that not only is it possible, but if you follow the advice here and put in the effort, it's almost impossible for you to fail.

- **They're afraid they're not a good writer.** Let me let you in on an industry secret: writing is just as much a science as it is an art. Like anything, talent and experience are assets. But they're not everything. You can learn how to write a good book.
- **They're afraid they'll fail.** Well, yeah. Welcome to being human, friend. Imposter syndrome is real. It's normal to doubt yourself, especially if this is your first book. If you didn't every now and then, we'd worry you were a psychopath. We've been doing this for a while and we still doubt ourselves. Fear of failure is natural, normal, and not a good enough excuse. But it does get in the way all too often.
- **They don't have support.** They jump right in, all by their lonesome, and get discouraged. It's not even their fault. The act of writing a book has developed a mythology around it. Someone holes up in a cabin or cozy desk somewhere and writes for hours on end and eventually produces something good. That couldn't be further from how good books are made. Without support, writers try, get discouraged, quit, and give up forever. Or perhaps worse yet, they write something they don't like and no one reads it.

To solve all these problems, there is actually just one simple solution: you need a plan. Good books don't happen by accident. They happen because the author has a plan every step of the way. They plan their idea, book structure, writing process, and publishing path. That's why Brittany succeeded. Even if you don't want a traditional book deal, to write a book people love, you need a plan. It's a lot to think about and requires work, so it's no wonder many of these books never make it out into the world. The saddest part of all is that these are voices and messages that we need, not reaching the audiences they're meant to. There are fresh voices out there getting left behind just because they don't know the process for creating a commendable book. But don't despair, this is a process you can learn! It's not rocket science, you just need guidance. Psst, here's another industry secret for you: all the best have help. That's where we come in.

Meet Liz

Ever since I was little, the only thing I ever really wanted to be was a writer. Sure, I went through the obligatory phases of wanting to be a tiger and then a ballerina and then a doctor like my dad. But from the moment I had agency and could think hard enough about my own life, I wanted to write. Like many in this profession (maybe you!?), it was a winding path to finally get here. There isn't a degree you can earn to show you how to become a published author or a three-step checklist to a creative career. After a few random and dead-end jobs postcollege, I finally landed a position as an assistant to a bestselling, traditionally published author.

While working for him, I got my feet wet in the world of publishing. I got to interview subject matter experts, research stories, learn how to write book proposals, and finally, ghostwrite a book for the first time. Without having much direction yet on what I wanted to do with my own ideas, ghostwriting became a lucrative way I could write books and gain valuable experience. It didn't take long before I had a six-figure freelance writing business, publishing connections, industry friends, and expertise. The journey involved lots of mistakes, late nights, rewrites, client calls, big swings, good cries in the shower, failures, successes, and incredible wins. And it led to an especially rewarding and collaborative career. In the last few years, I've had the honor of working with some of the biggest thought leaders and entrepreneurs in America. Oh and along the way, I also had two babies and lost a brother. It's been a lot. Wonderful and hard. Amazing and terrifying. A dream come true and devastating.

In the midst of all of this, something constantly nagged me. I regularly received requests from first-time authors to help them develop and write their books that I just couldn't take on. It broke my heart. One of the most gratifying things in the whole world is watching someone make their book a reality. I'm convinced there's nothing like it. It's part of what I was put on this earth to do. Saying no to these requests became intolerable, so I set out to find a way to help more aspiring writers finally write their books. One that didn't include the bottleneck of working with me one-on-one. I knew that plenty of people who landed in my inbox were determined and talented enough to do this on their own, they just needed some guidance.

It was around this time that, fatefully, Ariel and I met. It turned out, she had the same inclination. Too many ideas and dreams were dying on the vine because first-time authors suffered from both a lack of practical know-how *and* a mentor to cheer them on. Well, and a little bit because of publishing gatekeeping. But we'll get to that later. We set out to change that.

As writers, we naturally decided the best way to help more people was a book. This book. That clarity of what I wanted to do with my own writing finally came: I'll democratize my expertise and help others get published. This is the culmination of what I've learned from working with some of the best in the biz. And not just the publishing biz. As a ghostwriter, I've been lucky enough to write books for experts on public speaking, marketing, selling, starting businesses of all sorts, trauma, faith, and peoples' own personal stories in the form of memoir. And now I'm honored to spill my everloving guts about what I learned through all of that on how to write a fantastic nonfiction book to you.

Meet Ariel

It started with Nancy Drew. I loved her go-getter attitude, her undaunted spirit. She was measured and reasonable and brave, the perfect balance between her friends Bess (the voice of fear and caution) and Georgie (the voice of reckless daring). When I learned that Carolyn Keene, the supposed author of the Nancy Drew series, was not in fact a real person, but a pseudonym used by many authors collaborating together in an elaborate conspiracy to empower young girls like me, my heart just about broke open. *Anyone could write Nancy Drew.* Maybe—just maybe—even me.

I furiously wrote a series of mysteries and even a swashbuckling pirate romance story. But like many aspiring writers, I lost my confidence as I grew up. Occasionally, I would take out a notebook and furiously make an outline. I would catch a glimpse of a scene and record it as faithfully as I could. And then what? The butterfly would flitter away. I realized that I had no idea what I was doing. I saw that writing was hard work and often felt fruitless, whereas reading was always rewarding and fun. I saw that coming up with ideas and justifying what I had to say didn't come "naturally" to me, as I thought it must for "real" authors.

Instead of trying to solve these problems, I convinced myself that I wasn't a writer; I was a *reader*. Maybe, I thought, if I couldn't become an author myself, I could support the *real* authors out there by becoming an editor. So that's what I did. I got my first publishing internship, and then my second, and then my third—rapidly strengthening my editorial muscles under the patient and talented tutelage of my mentors. Then, I was hired at an independent publishing house, quickly rising through the ranks from editorial assistant to senior acquisitions editor. It was the dream job: scoping out exciting new ideas and prospective authors, negotiating contracts and flexing my people skills, and ultimately bringing books to life.

As you'll see in later chapters, much of the job of an acquisitions editor is saying "no"—even to authors you believe in, even to books you would desperately love to see on shelves, even to exciting possibilities you know could be realized if only the authors had a little guidance. Eventually I realized that I would love to say "yes" more. I could be the one to give them that guidance and teach them how to be successful. So I quit my dream job and I started a new dream: teaching authors how to ideate, plan, write, and publish books. I met Liz, and together we launched a podcast called *Hungry Authors*.

Throughout all of this, I continued dabbling in my own writing. I ran a book review blog for ten years. I started a newsletter, *Notes from the Editor*. I occasionally ghosted a chapter or a foreword for busy authors. I won NaNoWriMo three times. I started ghostwriting book proposals. I wrote my way *around* books for years, until someone asked me to write their whole book, and I finally had the confidence to say yes.

Once I was unleashed, I wrote six books in my first year of ghostwriting, including the first book under my own name, the one in your hands. And the whole time, I kept thinking, "Why did I wait so long to do this?" Whereas before I had felt stuck and mute, now I could not stop the words from pouring out of me. Like Ariel the Little Mermaid when she regains her voice from Ursula, I was singing again.

That's my wish for you, author. If you've been sidelining yourself, like I did for years, please take this as your cue: It's time to get serious and do the work you've been called to do.

You Can Write a Book

We wrote this book to help authors exactly like you. We're book proposal and planning experts. Ariel is a former acquisitions editor, and I'm a ghostwriter. You'll hear from us both throughout the book. We've worked with entrepreneurs, thought leaders, celebrities, business owners, industry experts, and speakers on their books and book proposals, helping them get six-figure deals and create bestsellers. We've had the privilege of partnering with some of the best agents and editors in the biz. We've helped people publish their books with the biggest traditional houses, the most amazing hybrids, and even just on their own. We know this process works and publishing your book however you want is possible. We see clients do it every day. Now, we're taking everything we've learned about what works and sharing it all here.

In case you're doubting, trust us: You can write a book. We believe in you. We're your coaches, and you've officially been drafted. Wait, actually this is a club, so I guess we're your club leaders . . . ? Nevermind. Mixed metaphors aside, you're in the right place. If you implement what we'll teach you here, this is what you can expect:

- **You will be confident in your idea.** There is a good idea inside you, you just have to find it and refine it. Good book ideas are usually the result of a process, asking yourself the right questions, and research. Some people might be lucky enough for the muse to show up on just the right day, but usually it requires some trial and error. In fact, after this, you might be able to come up with multiple good ideas because you'll understand how it's done.
- **You will prove to yourself that you can do this.** Belief in yourself is half the battle. Writing a book is a skill that you can learn, like anything else. And there's no better way to boost your belief in yourself than learning how and executing. This is called self-efficacy. We'll help you develop it.
- **You will know what will sell, and what won't.** One more time for the people in the back: selling books is good! Discovering what will sell and what won't isn't

quite as mysterious as it sounds. Before you type one word on the page, you can know what your audience wants, and ensure you'll deliver it.

- **You will have a path to publish.** If this book had an anthem, it would be: you don't need permission. If you want to publish a book, there are plenty of fantastic, high-quality ways to do that today, including traditional, hybrid, and self-publishing options. We'll cover all of these and help you decide which is right for you. And we'll teach you how to achieve them.
- **You will have everything you need to make your book happen.** We've done this with hundreds of clients: platformed or not, men and women, young and old, rich and not-so-rich, and it just plain works. We won't hold anything back and you can be confident you know what you need to write your book.
- **You'll also have two cheerleaders encouraging you and supporting you every step of the way.** We believe in you. If you're reading this, you're a Hungry Author who wants to write a book, which means you're our people. You already have everything you need: this book and your big, beautiful brain. (Well, and probably a computer would help.) You can do this! You got this. Writing a book is doable, exciting, fun, and worth it. Let's do it together.

Here's how this will work. This book is broken down into four parts.

Part I: Lay the Groundwork. Books that do well have certain things in common: they understand their audience, topic, and genre. We'll walk you through deciding on these and why it matters. This is the groundwork, and sometimes grunt work. It's the stuff that makes a huge difference down the line if done right. It may also require some patience, flexibility, and open-mindedness. Good ideas can take a little time to develop. But that's okay, it's worth making sure you've nailed it. We'll help you figure out when to refine your idea and when you've landed on it.

Part II: Map Your Book. Before you write a single word, you have to know where your book is going. In this part, we'll teach you how to structure your book in a way that connects with readers and makes your idea shine. You'll create a plan for each part and chapter so that when you sit down to write you'll know exactly what to do. Successful nonfiction books do this so well it creates seamless reading for the audience and the internal structure is hardly perceptible, as it should be! But we'll spill all the tea and show you how this magic trick works.

Part III: Write Your Draft. Coming up with an idea is one thing, figuring out how to fill a book with words is quite another. Writing is a job and you should treat it as such. This is where the rubber meets the road and your butt meets the chair. We'll help you set goals and hold yourself accountable, find the writing rhythms that work for you, and polish your sh*tty first draft until it shines. You're becoming a real writer now!

Part IV: Pitch or Publish. There are three possible paths to getting your book into the world: self-publishing, traditional, or hybrid. They all have their own benefits and downsides for aspiring authors. We'll give you the skinny on each of them and help you decide which one might be right for you. If you do want to traditionally publish, you'll need a book proposal, so we'll teach you how to write one. If you want to hybrid or self-publish, we'll show you what that looks like as well. Either way, you'll need to have a plan for marketing and selling.

Your publishing dreams are in your hands. At different points in this process, we'll present choices you need to make. We'll also share real world examples from our own clients and experiences to illustrate this entire process. There is no one path to writing a book; you can reach the same destination by many roads. We will give you everything you need to know and provide all the wisdom and information you need to make those decisions—but ultimately, they are your decisions. You have the agency and creative license, we'll provide the guardrails.

Brittany succeeded because she had a plan, that's true. She knew exactly what her idea was, how to write it, and how to publish it. But there is a deeper truth here that helped her achieve her publishing dreams: she had the right mindset. Because of that, she was always going to succeed. And if you apply what we teach you here, so will you.

You can do this. There's never been a better time to be a writer. Since mindset is the most foundational piece to that success, let's start there.

1

The Hungry Author's Mindset

The best piece of advice we can give to authors who *really* want to write and publish a book is this: Be hungry for it.

When I (Ariel) was an acquisitions editor, I worked with two best-selling authors who were nearing retirement. They had a successful line of books together, and they were looking for a next generation author to carry the torch for them—and they had someone in mind.

Julie was living in Bogotá, Colombia, at the time. Not the most promising candidate for a publishing company whose audience was primarily in the United States. She had a very small platform—a respectable-looking website, and a couple speaking engagements, and that was about it. On top of that, we weren't acquiring books on the topic she had proposed. Frankly, it wasn't going to work out. I went into the call ready to give her the bad news.

But as soon as Julie joined on video, I instantly liked her. She was warm and brilliant and, most of all—she was hungry. I told her my concerns, and she told me how hard she was working to overcome those challenges. Julie told me without hubris or conceit that she was making things happen. And I believed her. Our conversation was collaborative and problem-solving, and by the end of it, we had an idea for something that could work. Actually, it was a great idea.

With the promise of support from those two best-selling authors, I pitched Julie's new idea to my publishing team, and they let me take a chance on an unknown entity. Every editor takes chances like this sometimes, and many times they don't pan out. But occasionally, they do.

Julie was right about herself. She wrote an incredible book and started lining up international speaking engagements left and right. She pitched herself to podcasts in the United States, started an email list and grew it rapidly, became active on social media, and built a powerful network of other education influencers to help her launch the book. My team and I believed in her, too. We helped her make connections, pitched her to various blogs and online networks, and gave her as many opportunities to build her platform as we could throw her way. We signed her on for a second book even before the first book had published, because we could already see where this was going.

And guess what? With a lot of hard work from all of us—but especially from Julie—her book became a bestseller. So did her next book. And the two books she wrote after that. In the years since, Julie has never stopped building her profile and impressing the hell out of me. She now owns a successful education consulting business and travels all over the world with a team of her own trainers. And she continues to promote her books everywhere she goes.

The Hungry Author's Mindset

There's one thing stopping would-be authors from publishing their books, and it isn't their platform. We've seen authors with no platform get six-figure publishing deals. We've also seen mega-influencers with all-but-guaranteed book deals let their ideas languish in writing purgatory. What's the real difference between them? Their mindset.

In today's publishing climate, any author who believes in her message and has the gumption to try can publish her book. Here's what I knew about Julie the moment I met her: *She's going to do it anyway.* I knew that if I didn't say yes, she was going to go to one of my competitors, and then to a hybrid or self-publishing company. No matter how she published it, she was going to use her determination to succeed and her unstoppable energy to make that book as successful as she could.

Because the truth about Hungry Authors is that they will stop at nothing to achieve their vision. They have gumption, drive, and a certain *stick-with-it-ness* that compels them to keep going, even when the odds are stacked against them. It's not that they can't or won't listen to feedback; in fact, they *do* seek out and take action on the feedback they receive. They're willing to do the work necessary to make their book successful, and instead of seeing traditional publishing as the only way, they keep their eyes focused on the end goal: a great book. Make no mistake: A great book can be published in many ways.

We want to take you inside the minds of Hungry Authors so you can understand their perspective. The best thing you can do for your book—and for your career as an author—is to start thinking like a Hungry Author. Start saying the following phrases to yourself, and we'll explain why they work so well.

"I'm going there, and you can come with me."

Julie was, and is, the quintessential Hungry Author. Julie was going places, with or without me—but she was also kind, savvy, hard-working, creative, charismatic, and collaborative. I thought I would be a fool not to go with her.

There's something incredibly magnetic about that kind of determination and follow-through. It's not enough just to want it, even if you want it badly. You also have to show that you're willing to do the work—no, that you're *relentless* in doing the work—and that the work you do pays off.

Because the truth is, every editor wants to work with Hungry Authors.

Editors and agents have a problem. They want to discover the next Maya Angelou (*I Know Why the Caged Bird Sings*), or the next David Grann (*Killers of the Flower Moon*), or the next Robert Kiyosaki (*Rich Dad, Poor Dad*) *before* they become a household name. The problem is: How do you find such a wunderkind? Editors and agents receive *hundreds* of proposals from earnest authors who want it, and who truly believe their book is the next *Atomic Habits*—but the reality is, most of them won't sell. How do you find the true diamond in the rough?

Hungry Authors solve that problem by being willing to do the work.

Yes, every editor wants the credibility and prestige of working with big name authors, no doubt. But don't underestimate the potential value you can bring to the table, even if you don't have a large platform. You just have to convince an agent and editor that your book is going to be the astonishing success you believe it can be. And then you have to be willing to work your butt off to make it happen.

"Traditional publishing is not the only way."

Hungry Authors understand that the publishing industry is vast and constantly changing. Traditional publishing used to be the gold standard, but now there are many more options available—and those options might even be a *better* fit for their book! They keep their eye on the prize: a great book out in the world reaching readers. They let go of thinking that there's only one way to accomplish that goal.

This mindset is what will get you published even when you face a pile of rejections from agents and publishers. Hungry Authors don't wait for an invitation to the party; they're willing to host their own party if they need to. They'll pursue hybrid- or self-publishing without feeling like a failure, because it's *not* failure. In fact, as we'll discuss in part IV, hybrid- or self-publishing may be a better option for you depending on your "why" anyway. Hungry Authors are committed to reaching their destination, and they're open to exploring any path it takes to get there.

Remember: Success is not dependent on whether or not an agent or editor says yes to you; success is wholly and only dependent on your willingness to make it happen.

"I have a plan for success."

Hungry Authors don't throw fairy dust in the air and hope for the best. They are smart and strategic. They do their research. They make a *plan*.

There are two primary ways to go about writing a book: pantsing—writing by the seat of your pants, as it were—or planning. We're here to tell you that, in this case, one is *definitely* better than the other. We've seen too many authors start writing chapter 1 and get halfway through chapter 4 before they run out of steam. They come to us for help, and we have to tell them that it's time to go *all* the way back to the beginning, to set some parameters and helpful limits for the book, to figure out where the book is going and how they're going to get there.

When you're pantsing your book, it's easy to lose sight of the vision and the transformation in store for your reader. Making a plan ahead of time ensures that you'll always know what general direction the book needs to be heading, even if the route to get there changes along the way.

But planning isn't just useful for writing the book; planning is absolutely essential for marketing and launching the book as well. Hungry Authors don't just create something and then expect the world to show up for it. "If you build it, they will come" doesn't work here! If you build it, you've got to tell people about it. Hungry Authors plan in advance how they're going to tell the world about their message so it can reach as many people as possible.

"I'm open to feedback and willing to change my plans."

Julie started with one idea—an idea that she believed passionately in and *really* wanted to write. But from the publisher's perspective, it wasn't the right time for that idea. Julie held her goals and dreams for publishing with an open hand, and allowed them to change. A few successful books later, she finally did write that first book idea, to smashing success.

Hungry Authors don't stubbornly ignore the feedback they receive, especially from industry professionals with decades of experience creating books for their audience. Instead, they seek out new information, weigh it discerningly, and figure out how to integrate it into their plans. They view publishing as a collaborative, iterative process. The only thing they're *not* willing to do is give up hope and stop making progress toward their goal.

"This is just my first/second/third book.
I will write more books."

Sometimes, authors put *all* their hopes and dreams for writing on one book: usually, their very first book. That can be a heavy burden for your first book to bear! Most successful authors take smaller steps to publishing before they hit it big with their third or fourth or tenth book.

Hungry Authors know this, and they take a long-term view. They don't make their first book carry all of their hopes and dreams, and then declare themselves a failure when it doesn't do as well as they hoped. Instead, they focus on getting better and trying again. They know that each book is preparation for the *next* book.

And here's the biggest secret to the Hungry Author's mindset. Beyond focusing on *what* they need to do and *how* they're going to do it, Hungry Authors know something else that many other aspiring authors don't know: *why* they need to do it.

Know Your Why

One of the most essential questions you need to ask yourself is this: *Why do I want to write a book?*

Take a moment to write down some thoughts. After all, you're going to be doing a lot of writing in the near future. Might as well start now!

For most of us, the value of writing a book feels self-evident. *Because who* doesn't *want to write a book?!*, you might be thinking. But we encourage you to think deeper about this question. What do you hope will be different for you after writing this book? How do you imagine your life might change after writing it? When we shift the question a little bit, we can start to unpack our perhaps hidden motivations.

Knowing your why is critical to your long-term success and the foundational key to the Hungry Author's mindset. We spend a lot of time with writers helping them connect with their underlying motivations, adjusting their expectations for themselves and their publishing journey, walking them through battles with self-doubt and imposter syndrome, encouraging them, and pumping them up. That's where we need to start for you, too!

So let's dive deeper into that most fundamental why: Why write a book at all?

So many people want to write books—up to 80 percent of the population, depending on which sources you ask—that it's almost taken for granted that writing a book is something you should do. And we don't disagree. But you don't want to start this process because you think society demands that thou shalt write a book!

No, writing a book has to come from your own agency, because it's going to require a lot from you. You've got to believe that it's going to be worth it. Let's talk about some of the most common reasons people write books. Keep in mind: There are no wrong answers here. All of these are fine and valid reasons. And no matter what your motivation is, we have noticed that the more deeply felt your "why" is, the longer it'll sustain you in the process and the more you'll enjoy the experience.

People write books to:

- Share their idea/message with the world
- Tell an important story from their life
- Help others solve a problem
- Leave a legacy and record of history for future generations
- Prove to themselves they can do it
- Diversify their product offerings, if they have a business
- Grow their brand
- Get speaking engagements

It's likely that more than one of these reasons, or another reason altogether, resonates with you—and that's ok. But, if we're being really honest, one of them usually rises to the top as your *most* meaningful motivation for writing a book. You might need to spend some time thinking about which of these goals is most important to you.

We're going to keep coming back to this fundamental "why" throughout this process, because at the end of the day, your answer is going to be the driver that keeps you heading in the right direction. It's going to urge you to get back up when writer's block or self-doubt knocks you down. Your why is going to make planning your book, writing your book, and talking about your book so much easier in the long run. It is your destination—the light that will keep you moving in the right direction.

Stay Hungry, My Friends

It's likely if you're reading this book, you already are a Hungry Author. Your hunger and determination to get published is what's driven you here, and it will keep you going strong throughout the next sections of the book.

Obviously, hunger alone can't get you everything you want. You also have to do the work. The first step to publishing a great book is being able to answer some fundamental questions about your idea—that's up next in part I. We'll help you find your audience, choose a topic, and decide the right genre for your book.

You're going places. We're coming with you.

Part I

LAY THE GROUNDWORK

One of the biggest myths around writing is that authors get a wonderful idea and then sit down to write a book. Inspiration strikes and boom, you're banging away on the keyboard communicating your brilliant ideas into book form for the masses. This couldn't be further from the way true professionals do it. (No pantsing, remember?) If you want to write a book that makes an impact and changes readers' lives, there are many steps you need to follow between ideation and sitting down to write. And a few questions you must be able to answer.

What kind of book is this in the first place? What is your book about? Who is it for? What shelf will it sit on? What other books is it like? What promise does it make to the reader? If you have trouble answering these questions, buckle up, friend, because this is where the foundational work happens. Before we can get into mapping out your book, writing it, and sending it off into the big, wide world of publishing, there are a few things you need to get straight. Welcome to part I.

Here we're going to guide you through identifying your readers, clearly articulating your book idea, and understanding your manuscript's place in the market. Much like building a house, you need a solid foundation. If you don't have sharp, informed answers to the questions above, you're building your house on sand. And we all know what happens when that's the case. It won't take long before it all inevitably comes tumbling down when things get windy (i.e., you sit down to write). Nothing works if this part doesn't.

2

Pick Your Genre

When you write a book, you make a pact with the reader. That pact is:

> You (reader) will give me approximately twenty to thirty dollars of your hard-earned money and several hours' worth of attention, valuable time that could be spent playing with your kids or making money or planting vegetables or sleeping or zoning out in front of the TV. And I will make it worth it.

Readers buy a book expecting whatever the book seems to promise them. And whether it feels "worth it" to the reader depends on how well the book delivers on that promise.

So the real question is: *What are you promising to your readers?*

This is the power of genre at work in our reading and writing lives. A genre is a set of hidden promises that a book makes to readers. In the stellar guide to writing fiction, *The Story Grid*, by Shawn Coyne, he writes: "A genre is a label that tells the reader/audience what to expect. Genres simply manage audience expectations."[1] Genres are simply categories—buckets for holding ideas and conventions. And each genre has its own conventions that govern reader expectations.

We find, to our surprise, that genre is rarely talked about, even in writing and publishing circles—and yet, it is an unseen force that dictates so many of our reading and writing decisions. You'll sometimes find genre referenced in fiction circles, but in nonfiction it seems to be assumed that everyone knows and understands the different categories of nonfiction books and what they promise to readers. From working with hundreds of authors over the years, we can assure you that's not the case!

If you want your book to be read by anyone besides yourself, then it's a good idea to know what your reader will be expecting. Does that mean you can never defy readers' expectations in a way that surprises and delights them? You might be thinking of a book that enthralled you with its daring, or you might be someone who likes to buck convention and break the mold. Go for it! Be a rebel! But, like a musician who learns how to improv *after* they've learned their scales, you must know what the rules are in order to break them skillfully.

Plus, for first-time authors especially, understanding genre can give you a head start on writing the bestseller that we know you want to write. Genre can help with:

- Positioning your book effectively, so that you don't have to spend time explaining to potential readers what it is; they'll already know and be ready to buy it!
- Providing a template and guardrails for you to follow— like learning to color within the lines.
- Determining the type of transformation that will unfold throughout your book (which we'll talk more about in part II).
- Setting publishers' and booksellers' expectations, if you hope to traditionally publish your book (coming in part IV).

On the other hand, we've seen over and over again that when authors *don't* know the conventions of their genre, or haven't even decided what genre they want to write in the first place, they spend a lot of time creating something that ultimately won't serve readers' needs. In *The Story Grid*, Shawn Coyne writes, "Knowing genre is the single best way to avoid doing a helluva lot of work for naught."[2]

Ok, we've sold you on genre. Now let's get to the goods.

A Simple Guide to Nonfiction Genres

So what are the different nonfiction genres? You might be thinking that there is much crossover between genres—and you're right. Just because a book is prescriptive nonfiction doesn't mean it's not creative, and just because a book is creative doesn't mean it can't teach you something. The terms "prescriptive nonfiction," "creative nonfiction," "fiction," and all other genre names are just labels that we all agree to use when we're referring to certain types of books.

Like the folders on your computer, genres can hold lots of subcategories within them as well. Table 2.1 shows the most common commercial nonfiction genres and their subcategories—that is, the nonfiction genres you'd most commonly see for sale at bookstores. In this book, we want to help you understand the characteristics of the most popular commercial nonfiction subgenres, the ones that we help authors write most often. Though there are more subgenres than you see listed in table 2.1, the others all have their own conventions and would take many more books to write about! Each subgenre can also cover a multitude of topics wide enough to be their own unique *sub*-subgenres, like business, education, leadership, finance, parenting, and so on. Ultimately, though, even books around these topics tend to follow the conventions we've outlined here.

Table 2.1.   Commercial Nonfiction Genres and Subgenres

Genre	Prescriptive Nonfiction	Creative Nonfiction
Goal	To help readers achieve a transformation in what they know, how they think, and/or what they do.	To tell a story of transformation in the author's or someone else's life.
Subgenres	• thought leadership • self-help	• memoir • narrative nonfiction

Prescriptive Nonfiction

Prescriptive nonfiction is a broad category of nonfiction book that aims to guide the reader through a very specific transformation. These books inform or instruct the reader, and they can be written on a variety of topics. For example, the book you're reading is a self-help guide to writing and publishing for aspiring nonfiction authors.

What readers will be expecting:

- Exposition, meaning the author takes the time to fully explain ideas, theories, or techniques
- A logical, consistent organization that feels intuitive to the reader
- Chapters that follow an established pattern or rhythm
- The use of stories, anecdotes, and illustrations to depict ideas
- The use of second-person ("you") to address the reader directly

(Check us on this: Does this book meet all those expectations?)

Within prescriptive nonfiction, different subgenres typically follow the above conventions, but also come with their own distinct and unique expectations. In this book, we'll focus on thought leadership and self-help as they're the most common subgenres we get asked about. Other prescriptive nonfiction genres exist—such as cookbooks, daily books, textbooks, reference manuals, and other professional texts—but the audiences for those books are niche and the conventions are often dictated by specific associations, academic institutions, and publishers.

Thought Leadership

Thought leadership books break new ground; they often reveal exciting new research or theories that have yet to be understood and adopted widely. The explicit goal of thought leadership books is to permanently change not just the individual reader's thinking, but potentially our entire understanding of a field of study or thought. They do this typically by employing data, anecdotes, and comprehensive analysis of various arguments and ideas related to the topic. It can take a long time to convince someone of a new idea, so these books often (though not always) have higher word counts to allow the author enough space to accomplish that goal.

Because of these conventions, thought leadership books commonly cover topics like leadership, psychology, and the sciences. Good examples of best-selling thought leadership books include:

- *Mindset: The New Psychology of Success* by Carol Dweck
- *Caste: The Origins of Our Discontents* by Isabel Wilkerson
- *Start with Why: How Great Leaders Inspire Everyone to Take Action* by Simon Sinek
- *The Body Keeps the Score: Brain, Mind, and Body in the Healing of Trauma* by Bessel van der Kolk
- *The Song of the Cell: An Exploration of Medicine and the New Human* by Siddartha Mukherjee

You can probably think of others as well! These books have changed the landscape of public thought around their topics, leading us all to a deeper understanding of ourselves and the world around us.

Self-Help

Self-help books, on the other hand, focus more narrowly on helping the individual change something in their lives. Often, the reader already knows that they *should* change; the author doesn't have to spend as much time convincing them of a truth. Instead, what the author offers is a novel and easier *way* of accomplishing that change. Often, they offer a practical and straightforward set of instructions, accompanied by inspiring stories, to help motivate and guide the reader toward that change. Because of that, the author can take a more personal, casual approach to teaching the reader—although, ethically, we hope that an author would never offer advice that isn't backed up by solid evidence!

Keep in mind that whenever a reader picks up a self-help book, it's almost always because they're hoping that the book will help them solve a problem they're facing. Readers are therefore often disappointed if that book doesn't offer *enough* practical advice that they can begin to implement almost right away. Too many stories or vague generalizations can frustrate the reader who just wants straightforward help.

Some people don't like the term "self-help" because it sounds navel-gazing or self-centered. Feel free to use "personal development," "personal growth," or "self-improvement" instead; just know that all of those terms are talking about the same basic type of book and will follow the same conventions.

Self-help books exist on a variety of topics, including everything from bicycle maintenance to meditation, from potty-training your toddler to starting a new business, or from recovering from addiction to forging a new career. Self-help books can be secular or religious in nature; in fact, "Christian living" is a popular subgenre of self-help within religious publishing.

Popular self-help books that you've undoubtedly heard of are:

- *Atomic Habits: An Easy & Proven Way to Build Good Habits & Break Bad Ones* by James Clear
- *How to Win Friends and Influence People: The Only Book You Need to Lead You to Success* by Dale Carnegie
- *The Life-Changing Magic of Tidying Up: The Japanese Art of Decluttering and Organizing* by Marie Kondo
- *You Are a Badass: How to Stop Doubting Your Greatness and Start Living an Awesome Life* by Jen Sincero
- *The Purpose-Driven Life: What on Earth Am I Here For?* by Rick Warren

Perhaps you've read a few of these, or others like them. This is a popular subgenre, for both readers and writers. If you're here wanting to write this type of book, think about what you've enjoyed about other self-help books, what you didn't like, the reasons you picked up that book, and how it did or didn't meet your expectations. You're already starting to think like an author!

Creative Nonfiction

Creative nonfiction is a narrower category of nonfiction, characterized by its reliance on a central narrative (story) to convey a sense of transformation. These books use true-to-life stories to convey a theme or illustrate an idea. They are not focused on the reader's transformation (although, paradoxically, readers *can* be transformed from reading creative nonfiction!); rather, they're here to tell a story and hope the reader enjoys it or learns something from it. The possible subjects for these books are as limitless as our lives; we've read creative nonfiction about a scrappy racehorse (*Seabiscuit*), an escape from abuse and delusion (*Educated*), the recovery of a marriage (*How to Stay Married*), and a dozen other interesting, story-worthy, real-life events.

What readers will be expecting:

- The use of true, factual events and primary sources as material
- The arrangement of these events into a narrative arc, or storyline
- Storytelling techniques like beginning *in medias res* to entice the reader and hold their attention throughout the narrative
- The use of first person ("I" for memoirs and autobiographies) or third person ("he/she/they" for narrative nonfiction and biographies) point of view

Conventions-wise, creative nonfiction has more in common with the genre fiction than with prescriptive nonfiction, with the important distinction that creative nonfiction draws its stories from true, real-life events and experiences while fiction draws its stories from the author's imagination. Creative nonfiction does *not* mean that you get to "create" dialogue, scenes, events, characters, or any other elements of the story; rather, absolutely everything in your book must have actually happened in real life. The "creative" part of this genre is the narrative style and structure you bring to telling the story (more on that in chapter 7).

The two most popular subgenres of creative nonfiction are memoir and narrative nonfiction.

Memoir

Memoir is the recounting of an author's transformation through a specific event or scenario in their lives. Memoirs do *not* cover the author's entire life (that would be autobiography); as William Zinsser writes, "memoir assumes the life and ignores most of it."[3] In memoir, authors have the freedom to explore not only what happened to them, but also how they felt about it. Often, authors want to write memoir to process a traumatic hurt, and/or to share their story of healing to help others who have experienced something similar. They can be written chronologically or use storytelling techniques like flashbacks to engage the reader.

There's a lot of misunderstanding around memoir. Sometimes authors tell us that it would be selfish to write a story all about themselves, or that they don't want to come across as bragging about their achievements—or conversely, they don't want to appear as a victim to their circumstances. We usually ask those authors to give us examples of memoirs that were selfish, or where the author portrayed themselves as either a victim or a braggart. Can you think of one? Those examples are hard to find! You might find them lurking in the bowels of Amazon, with one-star ratings. But most of the memoirs we find at bookstores and on bestseller lists avoid those pitfalls. The beauty of memoir is that you have all of the freedom in the world to tell your story how *you* want to tell it. Successful memoirs are made by storytellers who attract readers with the quality of their voice. If you don't want to come across as a jerk, don't write like one! In fact, the voice with which you tell your story could be funny and self-deprecating, or solemn and sacred—whatever you want it to be.

Actually, memoirs can inspire and transport us into new worlds made all the more fascinating because they are *true*. Nothing is made up. That can be tricky to pull off for a few reasons that we'll discuss in part III on Writing, but make no mistake a memoir is a worthy and empowering endeavor for any writer. And no, you do *not* have to be a celebrity to write one!

The myth about celebrity memoirs comes from the fact that most celebrities (if they write a book) write memoir, but that doesn't mean that all memoirs are written by celebrities. In 2022, author and publishing expert Jane Friedman wanted to see for herself what kinds of authors received traditional publishing deals for memoir. Was it really mostly celebrities? She analyzed about six months' worth of memoir deals and found that, in fact, only 22 percent of those deals were signed by celebrities! The rest came from a mix of others with notable platforms, authors with an interesting media angle, established writers, and "others" (23 percent). That "others" category includes first-time authors and authors with no platform—in other words, people who simply have an incredible story to tell and the writing chops to tell it!

You've likely read a few of these best-selling memoirs:

- *Eat, Pray, Love* by Elizabeth Gilbert
- *Between the World and Me* by Ta-Nehisi Coates
- *I Know Why the Caged Bird Sings* by Maya Angelou
- *Educated* by Tara Westover
- *Crying in H Mart* by Michelle Zauner

When you look at this list, it's easy to see the incredible gift that authors can give to the world when they decide to tell their story.

Narrative Nonfiction

Narrative nonfiction is a story about someone(s)/something/ some event *not* written by the subject. It's also not an exhaustive accounting of the subject's life (that would be biography); it's limited to a certain period of time in which something interesting happened. The story is told with all of the same flair as fiction or memoir, usually with a narrative arc and the use of literary devices like flashbacks, imagery, suspense, and so forth to keep the reader engaged and entertained. Narrative nonfiction is real life that reads like fiction. (Just remember: *Everything* you include must have really happened, and/ or be verifiable by primary sources!)

Narrative nonfiction has become increasingly popular in recent years, with the help of "true novels" like:

- *Seabiscuit* by Laura Hillenbrand
- *The Boys in the Boat* by Daniel James Brown

- *The Radium Girls* by Kate Moore
- *The Bomber Mafia* by Malcolm Gladwell
- *The Library Book* by Susan Orlean

Breaking Genre Conventions

We know what you're thinking. "Yeah, but . . . do I *have* to follow these conventions?" In other words, is genre *prescriptive* (you should do it this way) or *descriptive* (most people do it this way)?

Genre is definitely *descriptive*, not *prescriptive*. But when you break the mold of what most other authors in that genre are doing, you are taking a risk. You have to be willing to accept that the risk might not pay off. You accept the fact that some people (maybe most people) will not like it. You accept that some agents and publishers will reject it because they don't have faith that what you're offering will feel like a worthy trade-off for readers' money and attention. You accept that even if you find an agent and publisher who will champion it, or you decide to publish it on your own, some readers will not appreciate it. You accept that you are embarking on an uphill battle, and you might lose.

But you might also win.

Breaking the conventions of genre can be surprisingly delightful and intriguing—as poet Maggie Smith (no, not the actress) did in her divorce memoir *You Could Make This Place Beautiful*. This memoir is a blend of poetry, a metanarrative of her own writing process, *and* the story of What Happened in her marriage. There are a few negative reviews for the book expressing disappointment in the writing style, calling it "disjointed," but for the most part, this book's Amazon and Goodreads pages are filled with glowing endorsements from readers who felt the unpredictable writing style reflected the realness of what it's like to go through a divorce. In other words, the unconventional writing style didn't detract from the message and purpose of the book; it skillfully supported and enhanced it. The risk paid off because Maggie is an experienced writer and knew exactly what she was doing.

If you want to break the bounds of genre, make sure you know what you're doing.

Mix and Match Genres

Once, I (Ariel) taught an online course on book planning to a writing group. We were talking about genre and one of the participants told me her bold and daring plan to write each chapter of her book in a different genre. It would be a mashup of fiction, history, self-help, and memoir, all rolled into one. I blinked at the screen. Each chapter a different genre?

"I've never seen any book like it!" she declared, enthralled by her own brilliance. *Yeah, there's a reason for that,* I thought. I knew this woman was working on a book proposal and she had said in previous meetings that she was determined to be traditionally published.

Gently, I told her that sometimes the reason we don't see anything like what we envision on the market is because there's actually not a market for it. We have boundaries and limitations in place for a reason—because those boundaries help us create something that readers will buy.

Authors often want to know how to blend genres together in a way that makes sense, and it *is* possible. The most common mashup is self-help and memoir, sometimes called a "teaching memoir." This happens when authors want to write the story of a challenge they overcame in their lives and include some explicit guidance for readers about how to overcome the same kinds of challenges in their own lives. These teaching memoirs might cover topics as specific as healing a broken relationship or as broad as becoming more resilient or embracing your creativity.

The general rule is: When you want to blend *any* prescriptive nonfiction genre with any creative nonfiction genre, the prescriptive nonfiction genre takes precedence.

Why? Because readers are selfish. And we say that with the utmost love and respect for them; it's just a fact. All of us are. When we pick up a book that promises to teach us something, we don't want to have to do the hard work of translating the authors' experience to our own lives! We want the author to do that for us. So, as authors, what does this look like? Ideally, this looks like writing the book to your reader, structuring it first and foremost as a self-help book, following all the conventions of the self-help genre listed above, and then using your own story to illustrate the key points you want to make.

One of my (Ariel's) clients, Meg Geisewite, wrote a beautiful teaching memoir about her journey to overcome gray-area drinking called *Intoxicating Lies: One Woman's Journey to Freedom From Gray-Area Drinking*. When I was working with Meg, we talked a lot about not just her own transformation, but also what her *readers* (mostly middle-aged moms) would need to make the same transformation possible in their own lives. Meg shared her own story, but she always kept the reader top of mind. She still followed all the prescriptive nonfiction conventions like using the second person point of view ("you") to address the reader specifically throughout the book and sharing relevant research and exposition *in addition to* her own story.

If you're thinking you want to write a teaching memoir, ask yourself if you can honestly make that commitment. Can you commit to prioritizing the *reader's* transformation above your own?

Often writers tell us that yes, they can commit to doing that. And then they start writing and what comes out is . . . memoir. Then they squeeze a little bit of teaching in at the end of each chapter, slap some reflection questions on there, and try to convince themselves (and publishers) that it's self-help.

Readers (and publishers) will see right through this, and they will NOT be happy.

When readers are disappointed by prescriptive nonfiction books, it's almost always because they weren't prescriptive enough. When readers are disappointed by creative nonfiction books, it's almost always because the storytelling wasn't exciting or interesting enough. Recognize that the goals of these overarching genres are very different. Don't let your creative thinking steer you off track here. It's better to do a great job satisfying readers' expectations with one genre than doing a mediocre job doing something "different" just because.

Make Your Choice

Before moving any further, it's time for you to decide. Hopefully by now you already have a good idea of what genre your book fits. If not, here are some questions to help you out:

- Do you want to explicitly help your readers achieve a change in their life, or do you want to tell an incredible story? If the former, you're writing prescriptive nonfiction. If the latter, you're writing creative nonfiction.
- Do you want to change the way everyone thinks about something we all take for granted in our lives, or do you want to help your readers make better individual choices in their lives? If the former, you're writing thought leadership. If the latter, self-help.
- Do you want to write an incredible story from your own life, or from someone/something else's life? The former is memoir; the latter is narrative nonfiction.

With that decision made, you're ready to decide who your book is for.

3

Define Your Audience

Your book cannot be for everyone. There, I (Liz) said it. I know you may want it to be. I bet you could come up with a reason why almost every single person in the world could benefit from your book. And you might even be right. We can think of reasons why even nonwriters might benefit from reading this book about writing. There are nuggets in here about marketing and pitching and self-belief! It's for everyone!

Again, it's not. You need to be honest with yourself about that. If you set out to write a book for everyone, you're essentially writing a book for no one. Our friend Grant Baldwin explains it perfectly in his book *The Successful Speaker*. He uses this analogy to clarify picking a speaking topic, and it applies just as well to deciding on your audience. Let's say you sit down at a restaurant. The waitress hands you a menu that's about twenty pages thick. You begin to peruse and notice that there's a Chinese section, American, French, Japanese, Italian, Mexican, and even Indian. Are you delighted to be in a restaurant that serves any kind of food you can imagine? No, certainly not. You assume that a restaurant that has this many options doesn't do any of them well. They don't have a specialty. They don't know who they're cooking for. All of these kinds of food require different ingredients and training. How could the chef possibly know how to do it all with any skill?[1]

That's what your book feels like when you don't write for a particular audience. It doesn't feel like it's written for anyone. And nobody wants to write (or read) a book for nobody. When you see a clothing item that says "one size fits all," you probably think, "not likely." You want your exact size, right? So it goes with books. In this chapter, you're going to learn how to decide on your exact audience—your exact reader. It's our job as writers to form our book idea to attract the people who will benefit the most from it, and then champion and advocate for it. These people will be the apostles for your book, sharing it with their friends and creating a chain reaction of people who buy and read it.

So it needs to speak directly to them. They need to feel like you've come down from the heavens to solve their exact problem or offer them a life-changing gift. If you try to write a book that feels like a gift to every person on the planet, it's not going to have the focus it needs to cut through the noise and have the greatest possible impact. It's going to be so general and vague that perhaps no one will hate it, but no one will love it either, and that's a problem.

This is good news! You don't have to try and please everyone in the world. You can actually have a greater impact by focusing on meeting specific needs and talking to a specific audience. And knowing your audience has the benefit of helping the entire rest of this process. When you know your audience, it makes the rest of the decisions clearer and the writing easier. It becomes the filter to run everything through. Your distinct audience is those bumpers on the bowling lanes that I need as much as my two-year-old, keeping the book in line and headed in the right direction.

There are close to a million books published in the United States every year, and they're all competing for the same readers. That's a lot of noise your book has to cut through with precision. By targeting your book to a smaller subset of people, you'll be able to stand out and counterintuitively reach *more* people than you would if you tried to write for everybody.

When in doubt, view yourself as your target audience. Or rather, yourself of a few years back. The beginner you. We don't mean write for yourself like you would in a journal. That leads to naval-gazing and waxing on about things your audience doesn't care about. But you almost certainly have deep interest in or experience with your topic, right? Best-selling self-help author James Clear did this when he wrote *Atomic Habits*. Someone asked him on social media who his target audience is because his writing cuts across many topics. Clear answered simply, "The target audience is always the same: myself." When asked how that answer coexists with Clear's additional advice to "do what's best for the reader," he said, "I think about what someone needs to know to understand the topic fully. I start with myself, but think about how to bring a beginner along for the journey."[2] There's a good chance that you, too, are writing for a past version of yourself—writing the book you wish had existed when you were struggling. Kurt Vonnegut said, "Write to please just one person. If you open a window and make love to the world, so to speak, your story will get pneumonia."[3] Maybe that one person you're trying to please is you.

When Tim Ferriss wrote the mega-best-selling *The 4-Hour Workweek*, he had a very narrow focus. He was writing from his own experience to overwhelmed start-up founders who didn't know the way out of the cage they'd created for themselves. Tim said that he basically opened up a Word document and wrote as if he was composing an email to a good friend who felt trapped at his company and didn't think he could leave.

"He felt like he couldn't kill his baby, it wouldn't run without him, etc.," Tim said.[4] At this point, Ferriss *had* created a much more balanced and sustainable lifestyle after initially working fourteen-hour days for years at his start-up.

He wanted to help his friends and readers find the same peace. The incredible paradox of writing for someone specific, though, is that then the book spread in popularity to many people outside of that narrow demographic. This often happens when you write so personally. Many more people are able to identify themselves in your words because what is personal is universal. And to write personally, you must identify your specific audience.

Who Can You Serve BEST?

There are lots of ways to go about identifying your distinct audience. You probably already have a good idea of the general topic you want to write about, and again, we'll get into that in more detail later. The first and biggest question to keep asking yourself is "Who can I serve *best*?" Not "how many people can I serve," but who would benefit most from what I have to say?

Some people to think about might be:

- Someone like you, who is facing a problem that you once had or who has a story similar to yours.
- Your clients, if you're a business owner.
- The people who read your newsletter.
- The people you spend the most time helping or who ask you lots of questions.
- The people who comment on your blogs or send you emails.

Take a minute and brainstorm about all the people who might benefit from reading your book. It's completely possible that all these people would derive some benefit from your book—but keep in mind that you can't solve all problems for all people, so keep asking, "Who can I serve best?" Once you have an initial list, you probably need to narrow it down further.

Let's say you want to write a book about yoga. You've got your general topic nailed down, but there are a lot of possible audiences for a book about yoga. You could write to:

- Beginner yogis
- Advanced yogis
- Yoga teachers

As you can imagine, these audiences have very different needs. An advanced yogi might not need the in-depth descriptions or demonstrations that a beginner does. And someone who is just learning yoga isn't going to be looking to teach yoga to other people. They all have different problems and they need different solutions. So right there, you've got three possible distinct audiences to choose from, and there are probably many more you could think of.

I (Liz) once worked on a book for an absolutely delightful client who was dead set on writing a book that targeted both aspiring entrepreneurs and experienced CEOs. As much as I tried to tell him how different those audiences were, his mind was made up. As a result, the book was vague and confusing and needed multiple rounds of rewrites. Those audiences are just too different. Experienced CEOs don't need help deciding on their business name and aspiring entrepreneurs aren't ready yet to talk about managing five hundred employees.

Let's continue. From here, ask yourself:

- What am I most passionate about?
- Who do I want to do more work with?
- What would be my easiest win?
- Where do I have the most expertise?
- Which of these audiences will introduce the broadest number of people to my work?

If you're writing a book about yoga, and especially if this is your first book, then you might decide to write for beginner yogis, for a few reasons. If you're an experienced yoga teacher, then you probably feel like you could teach beginners in your sleep—that's definitely going to be your easiest win. You might also pick beginners because you want to draw in the widest number of people possible and introduce them to your yoga practice. Hopefully, a lot of those beginners will later become advanced yogis and then yoga teachers themselves, and they will always look to you as a mentor and someone they can learn from. If you get them as beginners, you might just get them for life.

If you're a highly experienced yoga teacher running yoga-teacher-training programs and retreats, then maybe you feel like you already have the customer base you want and your expertise is in helping good yogis become great yogis—so you decide based on your passion that you want to write for advanced yoga practitioners.

Whatever you decide is fine, and it might take some soul-searching and reflection. Don't rush this, because this is the MOST foundational decision that you'll make for your book.

Demographics and Psychographics

Another way to define your distinct audience is by their demographics and psychographics. Demographics are more obvious descriptors like:

- Age
- Gender
- Marital and parental status
- Race
- Income level or socioeconomic status

Tim Ferriss's intended audience was twenty-five to thirty-five-year-old men who live in Silicon Valley or New York and work at start-ups. He may have also had an economic descriptor like "making between $100,000–$200,000." These labels help to further target your audience and help place you in the mind of your reader. Continuing with our example above, if you decided to write a book for beginner yogis, you may even want to further define your audience as female beginner yogis. You could even target beginner yogis who are mothers.

As much as we've harped on narrowing down your audience in this chapter, I do want to offer a quick word of warning that it is possible to get *too* specific, though it doesn't happen that often. Ariel once had a client say he wanted to write a book on origami for Christian college leaders ministering to students who have PTSD. Wow. This person definitely got props for knowing their audience . . . except their audience was perhaps ten people in the entire world. That does not a legitimate audience make. If you want your book to sell, you need an audience big enough to buy it. We sometimes refer to this as a "Goldilocks audience," not too big and not too small. Your audience can't be "everyone who likes yoga" and it can't be "twenty-two-year-old yogis who own a poodle and live in Nantucket." The ideal audience is somewhere in the middle.

Psychographics go deeper and are often more helpful when it comes to the actual writing. Though publishing professionals might say demographics are important for defining target audiences in board rooms with marketing teams, psychographics are more important for creating an impactful book. These relate to your audience's attitudes, aspirations, lifestyles, interests, and opinions. Here are some questions to ask to define your audience's psychographics:

- What keeps them up at night?
- What are they googling to solve a problem?
- What relevant experiences have they had in their lives?
- What are their goals?
- What are their values?
- What do they do in their spare time?

Adding demographics and psychographics to our yoga audience might sound like: Female beginner yogis between the ages of twenty to forty who don't have time to get to traditional studios. These women have full, busy lives and are looking for a convenient, private solution to learning yoga that fits their schedule. They value their social life, work, and families, and want learning this new skill to be as convenient and affordable as possible. Now *that's* a writer who knows her audience!

Creative nonfiction writers, you will want to lean into psychographics when defining your audience. Since you aren't solving a specific problem or necessarily tackling a topic, your reader's experiences are especially important in how they will relate to you and your writing. The rest of the advice in this chapter is still applicable to deciding your audience, but if you've felt stuck until now, hang out here for a bit. Spend a little more time thinking about your reader's experiences. This is where you will really come to understand the audience for whom your book can make the biggest impact.

Now that you've nailed down the people you can serve best, it's time to understand where your book fits into the literary landscape and learn from those who have written before you. Keep reading, my friend. Things are just getting good.

4

Position Your Book
with Comp Titles

Your book does not exist in a vacuum. That might seem obvious to say; there are millions of other books out there, right? But not enough authors consider the publishing landscape and where theirs fits into it when they decide to write a book. Your book exists among the family of books that is your genre, and more broadly within the wide world of literature as a whole. And it occupies a specific place there in relation to those other books. It adds to a conversation already started by "such and such," completely disagrees with "so and so," and is a lot like "you know the one" but with a crazy twist. It sits on a shelf between two other books at a bookstore, not at random, but because someone decided it belongs with them. Whether you realize it or not, your book was heavily influenced by its predecessors and will influence those that come after it.

Discussing your book within the context of other books is the art of what we call positioning. Positioning simply means how your book compares to others like it in the marketplace. It's important to understand because if editors can't figure out the positioning of your book, they will not acquire it. And if you cannot figure out the positioning of your book, you won't be able to successfully talk about it or sell it.

Those books, the ones beside your book on the literal shelf and in conversation around it in the figurative publishing landscape, are what we call your "comp" titles. That's short for comparative, comparable, or competitive titles, and there might be even more names for them. All of these refer to the same thing: books within your same genre that are published within the last few years and have a similar audience to yours. They are books that your readers also enjoy. Do not get hung up on the terms "competitive" or "comparable." This does not mean that your book will be competing with them or constantly compared to them. We know that sometimes intimidates first-time authors. As Jennie Nash says in *Blueprint for a Nonfiction Book*, "You're not in competition with other books; you're in community with them."[1] If your book is similar to *Eat, Pray, Love*, editors will not expect you to compete with or be the next Elizabeth Gilbert.

There are two main uses for comp titles.

1. They show how your book fits into the publishing landscape.
2. They serve as a model for mapping and writing your book.

Let's start with the first one.

Your Case for Publishing Success

Your book is like other books.

Did something inside of you just squirm? Sometimes when I coach new writers, the idea of listing what other books are similar to theirs makes them cringe (or come up empty, and we'll get to that in a minute). Authors often feel like their book is different—maybe even a special little snowflake the likes of which has never been seen before and will never be seen again! But let me tell you, friends, it's not. And what's more, *you don't want it to be*. And neither do publishing houses, agents, or readers.

Literary agent Lucinda Halpern says publishing is a look-alike business. Publishing houses want to find the next James Clear or Elizabeth Gilbert. Traditional publishing is also a pretty risk-averse business. They want to publish books that they know, as much as they possibly can at the time, will be popular. They like sure bets. The way they make these predictions is by looking at what has been successful before and choosing projects they guess will sell similarly. They also want to see that there's a large community of readers out there interested in books like yours. So you want your book to look like other successful books. It doesn't make yours any less special, it proves that there is a demand for your topic and makes the case that your book will be popular. If the thought of self-promotion makes you want to gag, pay close attention here because, when done right, choosing great comps for your proposal or query letter does a lot of the heavy lifting of convincing others how awesome your book is.

If you are seeking traditional publishing, agents and editors want to see your book "in conversation" with others out there. We'll help you decide what publishing path is right for you later on. When you reference comps in your query letter or proposal, it doesn't make your project sound unoriginal. On the contrary, it strengthens your case by giving them a better sense of what to expect from your story and makes them excited to see your spin on it. Nothing can bring to life the description of your book like a great use of a comp title can. Publishing experts and readers who are interested in your genre will likely have read many of the books there. If I say, "My book is like *The Life-Changing Magic of Tidying Up*, but for kids," don't you now instantly have a pretty darn good idea of what my book is like without me having to say anything else? If you don't live and breathe writing and publishing like we do, this example might not land, but to industry insiders, we pitched *Hungry Authors* as "*The Story Grid* for nonfiction writers." If you've heard of Shawn Coyne, you know exactly what we mean.

Here are a few ways you'll use comps in your publishing journey to further show how your book fits into the publishing landscape—and we'll guide you more through this process in part IV when we talk about your publishing options:

1. In your query letter to help describe and animate your idea to agents.
2. In your book proposal to expand on why there is an audience for your book. Here you'll describe five to ten titles and go into more detail about the similarities and differences they share. More on this in chapter 16.
3. In your elevator pitch when quickly explaining your book in interviews and to readers.

In addition to animating your idea and proving its popularity, comps can also help show its profitability. When you submit your book proposal, behind the scenes, editors will draft a profit-and-loss statement based on your comps to project sales. Using just a couple of well-performing titles can make the case for acquiring it.

Your Guide for Mapping and Writing

Not only do comps make the case that your book will be popular by proving that others like it have been, but they also help you when it comes to putting your book together. In part II, we're going to get into how to map your book. It's amazing, you're going to love it. And before we get there, let me ask you a question: have you read any other books in your genre? Can you name one or two that were on the bestseller lists recently? Do you have a favorite? Or even one you really don't like? If you can't answer yes to any of these questions, we have a bit of a problem on our hands. You need to be reading books in your genre! If you're not and you set out to write one of your own, that's like a director making a movie without watching one in the last ten years. Like a teacher who hasn't learned any new instructional techniques or an architect who hasn't visited any buildings built recently. To write the best book possible, you have to study others in your field and learn from them.

In chapter 2 we mentioned that genres describe sets of conventions and patterns to meet the expectations of the reader. You wouldn't use a ton of personal stories from your own life if you're writing someone else's biography, right? But how would you know most of these conventions if you don't even read anything in your genre (besides reading our brilliant descriptions, of course)? You *have* to know what other books your readers are reading to know what they expect. Not only does it keep you informed about the publishing landscape and make you look like an informed pro to agents and editors, it helps you write a book that makes the impact you want it to.

Here's what we mean. Writing a book for the first time is hard. Everything is relative, and it's not like we're doing brain surgery over here. But if you've picked up this book we're going to guess that you have an understanding that writing a book is quite an undertaking and you'll need some guidance.

But what if we told you that there was a treasure trove out there of exact play-by-play examples of how to write your book that took 99 percent of the guesswork out of it? Because there is! Your comp titles! The other books in your genre that are popular! All you have to do is copy them.

Okay, okay, it's a little more involved than that. And we certainly don't endorse plagiarism around here. But we don't entirely *not* mean it when we say: just mimic what's already been done. In part II we're going to talk about book and chapter structure. We'll cover topics like what chapters belong in your book and in what order, and what material goes into those chapters and in what order. Of course, we'll discuss this within the context of your Big Idea (in chapter 5).

And an important and helpful thing we'll ask you to do is study your comps with an eye for these concepts. We'll ask you to not just read for pleasure, but for research. How did your favorite author open her book? How many chapters is it? How many parts is it? How did she start that chapter? What came after the first paragraph? You get the idea.

We'll say it again: your book does not exist in a vacuum and so you do not have to write it in a vacuum. You can use the incredible work that's been done before you as a template for your own masterpiece. When I (Liz) signed on to write the memoir of a successful multi-seven-figure female millennial entrepreneur who came from poverty, instantly I thought of the acclaimed memoir and Netflix show, *Maid*. Both authors were young, single mothers who were born into poverty and struggled to create a better life for their daughters. With grit and determination, they did it.

So, I read and studied *Maid*. Not just at the beginning of the process, but many times throughout when I was stuck. I couldn't figure out how to start the book, so I looked at how Stephanie Land started. She doesn't begin at the very beginning, but drops the reader into a pivotal scene first and then backs up. *Okay, that's a good idea. I'll try that.*

Later in the process, to avoid a "saggy middle" of the book, I reexamined some chapters midway through to see what Land does. Does she tell one story for three or four pages or keep the timeline moving quickly along? How does she alert the reader that time has passed or offer background on a person? *Let me go find a scene where she does that. . . .*

Do not get too wrapped up in the details and questions about planning just yet. Again, shortly we'll demystify the process of outlining and you'll learn how to put together and write a great book. What you need to know for now is that one of the best ways to understand how to do this is to carefully read the work of other writers who you want to emulate.

Remember, you've got a community of writers and books to learn from. Don't copy them, don't plagiarize them, and don't be them. But study them. Learn from them.

How to Find Comps

Now that you know how important comps are, let's wrap up with a few tips on how to go about finding and choosing them. There's not a lot of mystery here, so we'll be brief.

1. Search your topic in an online bookseller like Amazon. Ideally you want to find books with at least fifty reviews, mostly positive of course. And ranking within the top fifty thousand of all books.
2. Peruse an in-person bookstore.
3. Look at the *New York Times* and other bestseller lists.
4. What books do you already enjoy? Don't underestimate the power of just starting with who you're already reading.

Regardless of how you want to publish and what your author dreams are, we cannot overstate the importance of reading books similar to yours. It will give you a feel for what's been successful before and give you the incredible gift of learning from other writers. There is a gold mine of ideas, theories, structures, and inspiration just sitting on a physical or digital bookshelf waiting for you to dive in.

5

Find Your Big Idea

What sets a best-selling book apart from the rest? What makes some books spread rapidly just on word of mouth alone because people can't stop talking about it? And why are some books as powerful today as they were twenty years ago?

There are many factors that differ among best-selling books, but one thing they all have in common: they present one Big Idea. So, what is a Big Idea anyway? (Other than the opposite of a small idea.) A Big Idea is an argument centered around a timeless topic *and* a unique angle. Here's what we mean.

A timeless topic is something that will be relevant forever. At least for a very long time. It resonates deeply with people and they will continue to be interested in it indefinitely. Timeless topics are things like finance, love, relationships, parenting, habit-building, self-discovery, politics, and so on. For as long as humans are alive, there's a good chance we'll be interested in love, right? Topics like these, with proven interest and sales records, contribute to what's called a publisher's "backlist." Those are books that were published more than a few years ago. A book with "backlist appeal" means a publisher thinks it will sell well long after it's published. You have a much better shot at backlist appeal if you pick a time-less topic.

An example of an untimeless (too timely) topic might be something like "social media," since we're unsure if social media will even be around in ten years or look anything like it does now. That's why a lot of social media strategy books are billed as something more like marketing, networking, sales, or connecting. Those ideas are more timeless.

Now, it's not enough to have a timeless topic. That alone does not make for a good book idea. You also have to have a unique angle on this topic—something different to say that hasn't been said before. Or at least hasn't been said in the way that you're going to say it. A unique angle contributes something new to the conversation that is already going on around your timeless topic. This could be a "hot take," new information, a different kind of voice, or a combination of ideas brought together in a new way.

Let's take *Atomic Habits* as an example. Obviously, Clear's book is about habit-building, or more broadly, self-improve-ment. This is a timeless topic. Humans are always looking to improve themselves and, despite examples I'm sure you can find (and know) to the contrary, gain some perspective on why they do the things they do.

What sets Clear's book apart from other habit-building books is that most make the argument that the way to better habits is through self-discipline. Clear's argument, however, is that the problem isn't you, it's your system. When most of the genre is saying "here's how to fix you," he swerved and went the other way: "The problem isn't you, it's your sys-tem, and here's how to master a new system of tiny habits. . . ." (we're paraphrasing here). Clear has also said that his comp titles helped him identify his unique angle: "The fields I draw on—biology, neuroscience, philosophy, psychology, and more—have been around for many years. What I offer you is a synthesis of the best ideas smart people figured out a long time ago as well as the most compelling discoveries scientists have made recently. My contribution, I hope, is to find the ideas that matter most and connect them in a way that is highly actionable."[1] Talk about not burying the lede. He spells out his unique angle right there on the page in his Introduction. When searching for yours, try examining your comps for what might be missing, like Clear did. Perhaps that's exactly what you are meant to contribute.

Here's another example. Much of Jen Sincero's bestseller *You Are a Badass* is the same self-improvement information you can find in many other books of the same genre. (And we mean no disrespect; Jen has said this herself.)[2] Her unique angle is that she offers the same advice in a more accessible way without any therapy-speak or pretentiousness. It's self-help for the people who think self-help is dumb. Plus curse words. Which is attractive to her ideal audience.

To continue with our yoga example from chapter 3, maybe your Big Idea looks something like this:

"Yoga is great for building muscles."

"Yoga is for everyone."

"Yoga builds coordination for team sports."

"Yoga is best done in frigid temperatures." (That one's if you want to come after the hot yoga people.)

Creative nonfiction writers, you need a unique angle, too. Because you're never *just* telling a story. You're making a point about it. If you are writing about grief and you find humor in your story, perhaps your unique angle is "Grief can be funny" or "Humor can help you heal." Cheryl Strayed's *Wild* isn't just about hiking the Pacific Coast trail and grieving the death of her mother; it makes the case that you can find yourself again through trials and tribulations. In *The Radium Girls*, Kate Moore tells the harrowing story of the girls who worked in radium-dial factories during the first World War. It was a coveted job until they all started falling mysteriously ill. But Kate doesn't just tell their story. She proves to us that, united, we can all fight against injustices and ensure that our suffering is not in vain.

What we're driving at here is that the best books *make an argument*. They're not just about a topic, they're about your *point of view* on the topic. And that's what really makes for an interesting book. We agree with Jennie Nash who wrote, "Every book is, at heart, an argument for something—for a belief, a way of life, a vision of the future, a way to solve a problem, a way to make a friend, or fall in love, or raise a child or connect with your soul."[3] Our friend and senior editor at Baker Books, Stephanie Duncan Smith, loves asking her authors, "What's the boldest statement you can make about your topic?"[4]

So we'll pose that question now to you. What is the boldest statement *you* can make? What argument are you trying to make with your book? What's the thing you believe that you wish you could convince others of? For us, the Big Idea of the book in your hands right now is this: "Any author with a great idea, a boatload of gumption, and a plan can write and publish a kick-ass nonfiction book." That's our argument, the hill we're willing to die on.

Here's a word for those of you who aren't necessarily interested in a commercially successful book. Maybe your main reason for writing isn't to get traditionally published, or even for your book to be widely circulated. Finding your Big Idea is still a worthwhile endeavor. If you want your book to be read by anyone, even just a few people, having a strong argument will help you make decisions during the writing process and make the impact you're hoping for on your readers.

Here are some Big Ideas of popular books you might have heard of, in the authors' own words:

- *The Pun Also Rises* by John Pollack: "**All progress, ultimately, is the result of playing with ideas and seeing new ways of connecting existing knowledge in a way that the sum is greater than its constituent parts.** And making such unlikely connections is the essence of punning."[5]

- *Profit First* by Mike Michalowicz: "**The system for profitability we have been using since the beginning of time is totally stupid.** . . . If you aren't profitable, the natural assumption is that you haven't grown fast enough. I have news for you, people. You're completely fine. **You don't need to change. The old formula to profit is what's wrong. It needs to change.**"[6]
- *The Power of Writing It Down* by Allison Fallon: "**Writing is not some elite activity reserved for the uniquely gifted.** Writing is communication, self-discovery, creativity, spirituality, and self-expression. **Writing is the essential tool we use to find and practice our sense of voice.**"[7]
- *Eat, Pray, Love* by Elizabeth Gilbert: "**If your life has become a trash compactor, then you are allowed to try to escape that trash compactor, whatever it takes. By escaping your own trash compactor of an existence, you can revive, reinvigorate and reinvent yourself, almost at a cellular level.**"[8]

You might notice that these arguments are a bit wordy (we've taken them straight from the prose of their books), but can be refined further, as we've bolded above. At the beginning, for mapping and writing purposes, yours should look more like the bold—succinct and powerful. You can elaborate on it in the book if you want to.

How to Find Your Big Idea

Okay, so now that you know what a Big Idea is and why it's important, let's discuss how to find yours. And we do use the word "find" on purpose. Every now and then a Big Idea might hit you like a lightning bolt in the middle of the night, but more often than not, you'll have to go looking for it. That's normal! All serious professional writers go looking for a Big

Idea. That's part of the job. You might get the hint of one from the muse, or be inspired by something while you're out and about. But almost certainly the first idea (or first version of the idea) that strikes you won't be the one you end up writing about. Ideas often need to be tweaked and finessed as you figure out exactly what your audience wants, what you want to say, and how you want to say it. There's nothing unwriterly about going looking for a Big Idea. Plus, once you learn the techniques we'll teach you below, you might just start finding them everywhere!

Start with Your Own Expertise

This is the easiest place to start. What are you good at? What do others constantly ask you about? Do you have any formal or informal education in a specific area? What do you know that most of the world doesn't? In almost every scenario, we encourage writers to start with their expertise. Especially if you want to write more than one book. That's what we did with this book! Therapist Lori Gottlieb wrote *Maybe You Should Talk to Someone* from her own experience as a counselor and having been counseled for many years. Former FBI hostage negotiator Chris Voss used his unique expertise to teach professionals the fine art of negotiation in *Never Split the Difference*.

In what direction have your education and experiences been pushing you? Something as simple as noticing that people always ask you for fashion tips or how you got your dog to stop peeing on the rug might point you to what it is that you have to offer that is helpful and unique.

What Unique Experiences Do You Have That Others Are Curious About?

This is another great place to start. Sometimes our Big Ideas can be found in our own lives. This is often clearest for memoirs. Popular ones like *Maid, Know My Name,* and *Educated* are all about unique experiences these women had that naturally, others are incredibly curious about. But you don't have to have lived a rather extreme story for others to be interested in your life. Maybe you're an identical twin or raise butterflies or don't want kids. Your Big Idea might be hidden in the thing that you don't think much of, but others find fascinating.

What Are You Curious About?

Follow your own instincts! This is a fun one. So many genius books have been written and new discoveries made just because someone scratched their own itch. Writers like Adam Grant and Malcolm Gladwell are famous for this. If you are intensely interested in something, there's a good chance others are as well. Susan Cain wrote *Bittersweet* because she wondered to herself, "Why do we love sad music?"[9] and it sent her on a journey. Dr. Atul Gawande asked in his book *Being Mortal,* "What if the sick and aged are *already* being sacrificed—victims of our refusal to accept the inexorability of our life cycle? And what if there are better approaches, right in front of our eyes, waiting to be recognized?"[10] What questions do you have? What are you curious about? What do you wonder to yourself quietly while sitting on the bus? It might just be the key to discovering your Big Idea. Because you can guarantee, others wonder, too.

This is a particularly helpful strategy for memoirs. For example, Kate Bowler's memoir *Everything Happens for a Reason (and Other Lies I've Loved)* started when she was diagnosed with cancer and thought, "Why? Why is this happening to me? What could I have done differently? Does everything actually happen for a reason?"[11] Let the seemingly unanswerable questions in life guide you to go looking for answers. If you are wondering about something, someone else probably is, too.

What Do You Disagree With?

You don't have to be a natural contrarian for this to apply to you. Sometimes your Big Idea, and more specifically, your unique angle, can be uncovered simply because you disagree with common wisdom or discourse. Mark Manson's *The Subtle Art of Not Giving a F*ck* or John Comer's *The Ruthless Elimination of Hurry* both take on a common topic (caring and hurrying) and make the case that we should not do those things. These are contrarian and surprising takes, in that most of us assume caring and moving quickly are good things. Jeff Goins's premise in *Real Artists Don't Starve* is that many of the most successful creatives throughout history did find a way to make a great living, contrary to the popular "starving artist" mythology. Maybe your Big Idea can be found in a belief you heartily disagree with.

Find Surprising Connections

Steve Jobs said, "Creativity is just connecting things. When you ask creative people how they did something, they feel a little guilty because they didn't really do it, they just saw something. It seemed obvious to them after a while."[12] Some of the best ideas are wholly original because they combine two concepts. Jeanette McCurdy's book, *I'm Glad My Mom Died* combines humor and grief. *Eat, Pray, Love* combines travel and self-discovery. Perhaps your Big Idea lives in the intersection of two seemingly unrelated topics that you're able to combine in a unique way.

Be Willing to Go Somewhere That Most People Won't

Maybe you're the person who is just willing to say the thing other people won't. Maybe there's a hard truth that isn't being told, and you're the one to tell it. This might sound like "Making friends is hard," "Motherhood kinda sucks," or "We all have a drinking problem." This one won't apply to a ton of people, and be warned, it might get you some hate. But drawing a line in the sand is also a great way to find ravenous fans. Robert Greene's book *The 48 Laws of Power* is all about how to acquire power and domination over others. It has some very controversial ideas in it, and has even been banned by some prisons![13] The point of Greene's work, though, is not that we *should* coerce and manipulate others, but that the world is controlling us constantly and we should know how to protect ourselves. As many people disagree with his point of view, plenty more appreciate it. Greene is a *New York Times* bestselling author many times over and has lots of faithful fans.

Tips and Tricks

- Study reader reviews of similar books. Look specifically at the three-star reviews. These can be a goldmine of ideas because they were written by people who largely liked the book but found it wanting in some way. What's missing? Do you notice any trends? Is there a gap you find continuously coming up that you may be able to fill?
- Study book descriptions. (These are often written by marketing and copywriting experts at publishing houses. Learn from them.) Pay attention to how they've positioned the book and how they explain what it's about. You'll notice in most, they include the book's Big Idea. Here is part of the Amazon description for *Atomic Habits*, with the Big Idea in bold:

    "No matter your goals, *Atomic Habits* offers a proven framework for improving—every day. James Clear, one of the world's leading experts on

habit formation, reveals practical strategies that will teach you exactly how to form good habits, break bad ones, and master the tiny behaviors that lead to remarkable results.
If you're having trouble changing your habits, the problem isn't you. The problem is your system. Bad habits repeat themselves again and again not because you don't want to change, but because you have the wrong system for change. You do not rise to the level of your goals. You fall to the level of your systems. Here, you'll get a proven system that can take you to new heights."[14]

- Read Reddit threads. This can get a little messy and takes some digging, but there are Reddit threads for literally everything under the sun. Find one on your topic and I bet you'll find some comments or common questions people keep asking. Maybe the answer to them is your Big Idea.
- Mine your own content. We'll get into this in a whole chapter later in the book. Write down the stories of your life and what you learned. Try journaling. Ask yourself, "What's the lesson I learned from this experience that could help others?"
- If you have a platform, write or ask publicly what people like hearing from you. Never underestimate how your Big Idea could be hidden in plain sight just because to you it seems so normal.
- Read other books in your genre, like we talked about in chapter 4. You may notice patterns or obvious gaps in the market or find yourself continually thinking, "They never say this" or "I wish they'd say this." That might be your sign that *you're* supposed to say it.

Here are a few thought exercises if you're stuck coming up with your Big Idea.

1. New York literary agent Lucinda Halpern says to be timeless in your topic *and* timely in your unique angle. If you've decided on your topic, try tying your angle to the conversation happening around it *right now*.[15]
2. We said it earlier, but it warrants another mention: Try asking yourself Stephanie Duncan Smith's awesome question: "What's the boldest thing I can say about my topic?"
3. Jeff Goins uses the convention: *Everyone thinks* _____ *but the truth is* _____. This one's great for the contrarians among us.
4. Eric Nelson, vice president and editorial director of Broadside Books, said that people know the world is full of hard problems, and most of those problems can be solved by turning a dial. What he means is, the right answer is almost always doing a little more or a little less of something. But . . . that's a little boring. The best books teach us one clean step we can take to solve or explain a surprising percentage of the problem. "Think in switches, not dials," he recommends.[16] *No more gluten. Delete social media. Make your bed. Get up early.* These are switches we can flip for maximum impact in our lives.
5. Draw a line in the sand and force people to pick a side. Nothing is more powerful or potentially controversial than saying "this is right" and "this is wrong." And writers have been doing it effectively for years. Do you have a line you want to draw?
6. When describing what they look for in a book, we've heard agents say, "Tell me something I don't know about a subject I already love."[17] If you know a decent amount about a topic and you're writing for an audience that's interested in it, what's something they likely don't know yet?

Don't be afraid to take your time here. I know you probably want to get on with the writing process, or perhaps even came to this book thinking you already had your Big Idea. But we encourage you to think it through or even reexamine it. You have something unique to say. There's a conversation happening out there on a topic in the book world that needs your contribution. So, go find your Big Idea.

Part II

MAP YOUR BOOK

Imagine that you're setting out on a road trip. Would you hop in a car and just start driving? Or would you think about where you want to go and then plot a course in Google Maps to help you get there?

So often, aspiring authors start off on a "road trip" without a clear sense of where they're going, let alone how to get there—and so they end up wandering. In chapter 5, you identified your Big Idea. That's your destination. Now, in part II, we want to make sure you have a step-by-step map so that you arrive at your destination, especially since you're bringing readers along for the ride! Buckle up, friends. This is about to get really good.

A book map is a visual representation of your book's structure, with every part, chapter, and section identified. It is the secret sauce to a successful, impactful book that moves readers. This is what's missing from most authors' process. We don't want to oversell it, but it's kinda magical. If you do this part right, it's hard to write a bad book.

You can think of a book plan like the skeleton of your book, or the scaffolding. A good structure will ultimately be invisible to your reader, but we're going to teach you how to see the hidden structure in books so that you know how to create your own. This will become one of your author superpowers!

Book maps help you:

- Think about the details while keeping the big picture in mind
- Test and refine your Big Idea
- Identify where you have too much or too little information at a glance
- Understand the hierarchy of your content
- Create an intuitive journey for the reader from start to finish
- Always know what you need to write next

What a Book Map Looks Like

A book map starts with your Big Idea at the top, then clarifies the transformation for the reader, identifies any parts and chapters, and pinpoints the content within those chapters. Each level of the book map flows from the level above.

Figures II.1 and II.2 show simplified examples of what you're aiming to create, depending on whether you're writing prescriptive or creative nonfiction. If it looks like a lot of information right now, don't worry! In the next four chapters, we'll break it down for you piece by piece.

It's important to remember that the models and templates we'll share with you in part II are not meant to be cages for your book ideas; they're meant to be starting points. Remember from chapter 2: Once you know the rules, you can break them. The templates in the following pages show you how to follow the rules. They're a great place to start, especially for first-time authors, but don't get worried if you find your story or your content doesn't fit perfectly.

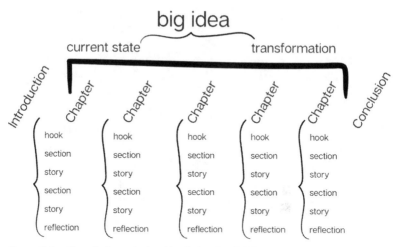

Figure II.1. Sample Prescriptive Nonfiction Book Map

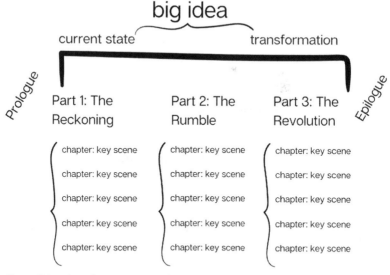

Figure II.2. Sample Creative Nonfiction Book Map

Use your creative genius to help you apply the information appropriately and feel free to bring the unique touch that only you can bring to your book!

What You'll Need

For the next four chapters, you'll want to have some materials on hand. You can do this process digitally using any software that provides a virtual whiteboard and sticky notes. But our favorite method is to do this analog style with *actual* paper and sticky notes! We recommend grabbing a pad of extra-large stickies (25" x 30"), a multicolored pack of normal-sized sticky notes or index cards (no smaller than 3" x 3"), and a handful of colorful markers. We'll explain what to do with them in the following chapters.

You'll also need a large space that you can come back to, like an office wall, dining room table, or extra-large window. We know from experience that trying to do this in a public space like a coworking space or coffee shop can be difficult because you'll want to take breaks and probably spread this process out over the course of a couple days or weeks. You don't want to rush your book map! If you don't have space at home, use a browser-based software like Jamboard, Mind-Meister, Figma, or Mural. Most of these programs have free trials that will allow you to create a few whiteboards without signing up for a paid subscription.

Are you ready for the first easy step? Write the Big Idea you came up with in chapter 3 on a sticky note and place it at the top of your designated book map area. If you're still unsure whether you have the "right" Big Idea (there's no right or wrong! Only experiments!), don't worry. By working through a book map, you'll be able to refine your idea and test to see whether it really works.

Then, when you're ready for the next step, turn the page. We'll start with your Transformation Tale.

6

Tell Your Transformation Tale

Most genres tell a story of transformation—what we call their "Transformation Tale." Prescriptive nonfiction books are about the transformation of the *reader*; memoirs are about the transformation of the *author*; and narrative nonfiction books are about the transformation of *someone* or *something* besides the author.

Literature professor Joseph Campbell documented the inner workings of classic Greek myths in his book *The Hero with a Thousand Faces*, showing how their principles apply to psychology and modern storytelling. He summarized the hero's journey as, fundamentally, a story of transformation:

> A hero ventures forth from the world of common day into a region of supernatural wonder: fabulous forces are there encountered and a decisive victory is won: The hero comes back from this mysterious adventure with the power to bestow boons on his fellow man.[1]

Campbell's insights have been used to understand and improve storytelling devices in fiction, psychology, and even marketing. In this chapter, we'll show you how to apply many of the same principles of transformation to nonfiction books.

The Hero

Every Transformation Tale has a few basic elements in common. First, every Transformation Tale features a **hero**. The hero might not be a Greek god or a knight in shining armor; often, the hero is in fact a bumbling fool or a prideful snark or a daring rebel. What makes them the hero of a Transformation Tale is the fact that, by the end of the book, they will have changed. If you're writing a memoir, by default *you* are the hero of your book—not because you pulled yourself up by your bootstraps (although you may have) or because you're so incredibly awesome (although you probably are!), but because by the end of the book, you will show how you've changed through a specific experience in your life. If you're writing prescriptive nonfiction, then your reader is your hero, because they will be making changes in their life based on the advice you give them. And don't get hung up on the term "hero"; we use it here because Joseph Campbell used it. But if you don't like that term, you can call this person the "main character," the "protagonist," the "subject," or maybe just "the reader" or "me."

Every hero's Transformation Tale has three basic parts: their **current state** (who they are at the beginning of the book), their **transformation** (who they become by the end of the book), and the **in-between** (how they get there). Transformation Tales look a little different for prescriptive and creative nonfiction books, so we'll share an illustrative story for each.

Prescriptive Transformation Tales

Meet Harley. Harley is your reader, and she's the hero of your book. (If you're writing a book for an audience of one particular gender, feel free to pick a typically gendered name and use their preferred pronouns to represent your hero! For now, we'll use she/her for Harley.) In your book, you'll be taking

Harley on an adventure, an adventure that will change her life for the better. As Jennie Nash describes, "They [readers] start out in one place: a place of being unaware or unsure or uninformed or uninspired. And they end up in another place: a place of knowing something new, understanding something new, embracing something new, believing something new." This is the journey you're creating for Harley.

Current State

Harley deeply wants something—whether it's something lofty, like a better marriage, or something practical, like an investment account filled with money so that she can retire early. We'll call this Harley's heart's desire. Her heart's desire is something deep and meaningful, something that helps her envision a better future.

But Harley has a problem. Something is preventing her from getting her heart's desire. This sticky problem is multifaceted and complex; she can't easily solve it on her own (that's why we call it "sticky"—because it sticks around). In fact, she's probably been trying to fix it for a long time, and her efforts have been fruitless. This sticky problem is a perpetual thorn in her side, and it haunts her. She's desperate to get this fixed, and she's ready for help.

What's important to keep in mind here is the weightiness of Harley's problem. We all solve fairly simple problems for ourselves every day. If I need a new toothbrush, I just run out to the store (or make my spouse go) to buy a new one. But that's not a book-worthy problem. What makes Harley's problem worthy of a book is the fact that it cannot be solved easily on her own. In fact, it's so complex, she may not even fully understand the problem she's facing!

Not only is Harley facing this sticky problem; it's likely that she's making it *worse*. If the problem she's facing is a crumbling marriage, she may not see how her attempts at helping her partner come across as criticism. She may not realize how her fear of risk makes her a bad investor. Harley is very aware of the fact that what she's doing isn't working, and it makes her feel discouraged, unsure that it'll ever get better, and maybe even hopeless.

This is the reader's current state: They have a sticky problem, they don't understand it, it makes them feel blue-y, and they're making it worse. You should already have a good idea of your audience and the problems they face from the work you did in chapter 2.

Let's take *Atomic Habits*, for example. James Clear's reader desperately wants something: better habits for a healthier, happier life. The problem is that most people use the wrong systems (mainly setting ambitious goals and expecting that their behavior will therefore change) to try to force those habits. When they don't work, his reader feels like a failure. So they either double down and just try harder next January when goal-setting time rolls around, or they give up altogether.

Yikes. His reader is in a pickle—and yours is, too.

The In-Between

This is where you, Author, come in to help. You have credibility; you're an authority on solving this problem. You see things Harley can't see. You have the knowledge, data, and resources to inform Harley about the problem she's facing and why her attempts at solving it haven't worked. You're familiar with the pitfalls that readers like Harley often face, and you've got a proven path to success. That path includes examples, stories, tools, steps to follow, and frameworks to instruct Harley on how to solve her problem so she can get her heart's desire.

Not only that, but you can share your information in such a compelling, intuitive, engaging way that Harley feels encouraged and confident to finally make changes that will work in her life. Don't worry if you don't quite know how to do this just yet—we'll teach you how in the next couple chapters!

All of this information—the examples, the frameworks, the steps, the case studies, the data—makes up the space in-between your reader's current state and their transformation. The in-between will comprise most of your chapters.

With all of that incredible knowledge and information just waiting at her fingertips, how could Harley *not* want to read your book?!

That's how many readers—over four million, according to his sales!—feel about *Atomic Habits*. Instead of telling his readers to have more self-discipline, James Clear identifies four keys for developing better habits: cue, craving, response, and reward. And he maps those keys onto "Four Laws" that are easy for readers to remember and apply:

1. Make it obvious
2. Make it attractive
3. Make it easy
4. Make it satisfying

He lays out a clear and clever pathway to better habits for his readers so that they can take immediate action and see immediate results.

The Transformation

The most important part of the Transformation Tale is that the hero is the person doing the changing. That means you, Author, are not the hero of this tale (this is especially important to remember if you're hoping to write a self-help/memoir mashup!). You cannot solve Harley's problem for her. You've given her everything she needs to solve it, but then it's up to her to actually apply all of your brilliant insights in her life. Your job is to make her *want* to apply those insights. It's kind of like parenting—it hurts when you see your kid fail to act how you've taught them, and it's also the most incredible reward when you see them do it! But as parents know all too well, you can't force your kids to do the right thing. Eventually, they have to choose it on their own. That goes for Harley and all of your readers, too.

So how do you make Harley *want* to do everything you've laid out for her in your book? You remind her of the transformation waiting for her. Show her a vision of what it looked like for someone just like her to solve the same problem and achieve their heart's desire. Remind her of her heart's desire, and how amazing it will be once she gets it. Remind her just how far she's already come; at the beginning of the book, she had no idea how to solve her sticky problem! Now she understands the problem *and* has a proven path for solving it. All she has to do to accomplish the transformation is take the next steps that you've given her.

James Clear lays it out pretty bluntly in the conclusion of *Atomic Habits*: "With the Four Laws of Behavior Change, you have a set of tools and strategies that you can use to build better systems and shape better habits. . . . The secret to getting results that last is to never stop making improvements. It's remarkable what you can build if you just don't stop."[2] Well there you have it, folks. It's that easy (and that hard!). We love that in these words, Clear tells the reader exactly what choice she needs to make: Will she apply all of the principles from the book and form better habits and systems, or will she continue to suffer in old systems that don't work? The key to a great prescriptive conclusion is in offering the reader that ultimate choice, and then trusting that they'll do the right thing.

And, Author, your job here is done! Exit stage left.

Creative Transformation Tales

If you're writing a creative nonfiction book, like memoir or narrative nonfiction, your book's Transformation Tale will still include the same three pieces (current state, in-between, and transformation), but they'll look a little different. The most important distinction is that with creative nonfiction, your reader is not the hero; if you're writing memoir, then *you* are the hero. If you're writing narrative nonfiction, your subject (whether it's Seabiscuit the horse or the Los Angeles Public Library) is the hero. For this illustration, let's call the hero Henry.

Current State

Life is constant for Hero Henry. It may be great; it may be sad; it may be boring. Whatever it is, it's stable. It's the norm for Henry. That life is what Henry knows.

And then Something happens—a catalyst. A family member dies, or Henry's spouse does something unforgivable, or Henry is diagnosed with a devastating illness. This is often called the inciting incident, or in Joseph Campbell's language, the "call to adventure." That normal life Henry was used to is disrupted.

Whatever that catalyst is, it is first and foremost an invitation for Henry to enter a new life, even if he doesn't yet know what that new life will look like. The catalyst is likely part of Henry's external life—his physical existence and his relationship with others. But the invitation to change is very much an *internal* one. A family member dies (external catalyst), and suddenly Henry realizes how precious life is and how he's been wasting his time (internal invitation). Or his spouse's actions (external catalyst) force Henry to realize he'll need to summon courage to get out of the relationship (internal invitation). The devastating illness (external catalyst) prompts Henry to understand his mortality in a whole new way and question the beliefs he held his whole life (internal invitation).

Often, Henry resists this invitation, because it's hard to break through the old habits. No one really *wants* to go through the hard work of changing. Eventually, though, in order for there to be a story, Henry will have to accept the invitation to this internal journey—whether he wants to or not. The external catalyst is so life-changing that there's really no going back. Truth has been revealed, eyes have been opened. You can't unsee what you've seen or undo what's been done.

At that point, Henry leaves his current state behind and begins his internal journey.

Think, for a moment, about one of the best-selling memoirs of all time: *Eat, Pray, Love* by Elizabeth Gilbert. Liz Gilbert's external catalyst is her divorce, but she's invited into the internal journey to know herself, to stop pretending to do whatever other people think she should do, and to live life according to her own terms. At first, she tiptoes around this invitation, going about her work, but with the addition of taking Italian lessons. Then she goes to Bali on an assignment for work and meets a medicine man who predicts that she'll come back to Bali soon. That's when she has the idea to finally *do* something.

The In-Between

Once Henry accepts the invitation, the journey begins. What's important here is that Henry takes *action*; his internal transformation demands external action. He doesn't just go back to work the next day and resume his normal life, but with the new flavor of feeling sorry for himself. He decides, finally, to *do* something about it.

The journey is filled with challenges and setbacks, with many hard lessons learned along the way. As Joseph Campbell wrote, "fabulous forces are there encountered."[3] But Henry has no choice but to keep moving forward. He perseveres through everything. He is tempted to give up many times—but, remember, he can't unsee what he's seen. There's no going back to his life before the catalyst, as much as he may want to. The only way out is forward.

This in-between of taking action and dealing with setback after setback comprises the bulk of Henry's story (your story, if you're Henry), and the bulk of your book. Through it all, we should see Henry progressing in his internal journey, slowly beginning to make different choices and becoming, essentially, a new person. He may have some help along the way, but ultimately Henry makes the necessary changes in his life—because he's the Hero.

For Elizabeth Gilbert, taking action meant planning a year-long trip to Italy, India, and Indonesia in pursuit of pleasure, devotion, and balance to discover who she is. Along the way, she wrestles with her internal demons (like loneliness and depression), but she continues taking action. In Italy, she goes back to school and eats incredible meals. In India, she practices yoga and learns how to meditate. And in Indonesia, she forms deep friendships and experiences the power of helping others. You can see how these external actions help her move forward on her internal journey.

The Transformation

The story ends when the hero completes their internal journey and becomes that new, improved person. Your hero's internal journey *must* resolve positively in order for the story to feel satisfying to the reader. This doesn't mean you have to have a *happy* ending; you don't have to force rainbows and butterflies if that's not authentic to the story you want to tell. Instead, the hero's journey might end with them finding justice, accepting responsibility for something they've done, or simply accepting what is. What matters is that their internal journey ends on a moral high note. External journeys, on the other hand, may resolve negatively, positively, or not at all.

Table 6.1 shows some examples of how this might look.

The transformation can feel difficult for some authors to find. Many aspiring memoir writers have said things like, "I can't write my story yet because it's still happening," or "No

Table 6.1. External and Internal Transformations

	Catalyst/Invitation	Transformation	Positive/ Negative
External	Parent dies	Parent is still dead	N/A
Internal	Stop wasting time on things that don't matter	Makes better choices and finds stability and happiness	Positive
External	Spouse cheats	Ends the relationship	Positive
Internal	Gain confidence and break pattern of codependence	Gains the confidence to be on his own	Positive
External	Deal with worsening illness	Dies	Negative
Internal	Resolve questions about faith	Faith grows stronger	Positive

one will want to read my story because it has a sad ending." If this is you, we want you to know that the only requirement for your story is that you've experienced a positive *internal* transformation. The situation that launched you onto your journey may not have ended yet, or may not have ended the way you wanted it to, but if you've become a better, stronger person through it—you have a story.

In *Eat, Pray, Love*, Elizabeth Gilbert's journey is complete when she realizes she is finally living on her own terms. She also has a new boyfriend—a positive external transformation—but that's not what really matters. At the end of the book, she writes: "I think about the woman I have become lately, about the life that I am now living, and about how much I always wanted to be this person and live this life, liberated from the farce of pretending to be anyone other than myself."[4] That's how we know her internal transformation is complete.

Don't Forget Your Big Idea

All of your book's content should flow from your book's Big Idea (figure 6.1), which we discussed in chapter 5. Your Transformation Tale is how you prove or illustrate that Big Idea. (It's also how you refine and test your Big Idea to make sure you like it and it works!)

big idea

current state   transformation

Figure 6.1.   Big Idea to Transformation

We like to break it down in a simple table, with your Big Idea at the top and the three parts of the Transformation Tale below. Table 6.2 shows what the Transformation Tale for *Atomic Habits* would look like. Keep in mind, this is our brainstorm version based on the finished book. If James Clear had created a Transformation Tale before he started writing, it probably would have looked a little different!

Table 6.3 shows how this might work in a creative non-fiction book, back to *Eat, Pray, Love*. The Big Idea is drawn directly from Elizabeth Gilbert's own words in the book.

Table 6.2. Example Transformation Tale: *Atomic Habits* by James Clear

Big Idea: The problem with your habits isn't you; it's your system.

Current State	In-Between	Transformation
The reader . . . • Wants to achieve certain life goals, but consistently fails • Doesn't have a system for unlearning bad habits or learning good habits • Feels stuck in bad habits and hopeless that change is possible • Tried many times to change habits before with no success • Keeps trying to force new habits without success	Four laws that will make changing your habits easier: • Make it obvious (cue) • Make it attractive (craving) • Make it easy (response) • Make it satisfying (reward)	• Has a system in place for ditching bad habits and adopting new ones • Makes steady progress toward goals • Focuses on the small, daily tasks that make change over time • Creates the right environment for change • Feels confident that they can set a goal and achieve it

Table 6.3. *Eat, Pray, Love* Transformation Tale

Big Idea: "If your life has become a trash compactor, then you are allowed to try to escape that trash compactor, whatever it takes. By escaping your own trash compactor of an existence, you can revive, reinvigorate, and reinvent yourself, almost at a cellular level."

Current State	In-Between	Transformation
External catalyst: Divorce	Liz travels to . . .	*External transformation:* New boyfriend!
	Italy in pursuit of pleasure	
Internal invitation: Discover who she is and live life on her own terms	• Takes classes • Discovers new foods • Fights loneliness and depression	*Internal transformation:* Living life on her own terms and feeling happy and free
	India in pursuit of devotion • Learns to meditate • Does lots and lots of yoga • Fights to love herself	
	Indonesia in pursuit of balance • Shadows the medicine man • Makes new friends • Fights to love others (including a new beau!)	

Map It Out

Now that you understand the three pieces of all Transformation Tales, we recommend that you practice mapping the Transformation Tales in other books before you try mapping your own. In chapter 4, we talked about comp books. Pick one or two of those comps now to work with. In the following chapters, we'll keep using *Atomic Habits* and *Eat, Pray, Love* as examples. Don't get hung up if the book you want to write is not exactly like one of these; we just want to illustrate the process for you. You should pick comp books that are more like the book you want to write so that you *do* have good models to learn from!

Q&A

Q: Do I have to read my comp books before I try mapping them out?
A: No, you don't have to read the entire thing; but you should be familiar enough with the content that you understand what the book is trying to achieve. We recommend you at least read the introduction or prologue and the conclusion or epilogue.

Get Your Materials Ready

If you're doing the book-mapping process manually, then get three of your extra-large sticky notes and place them side by side. If you don't have the extra-large sticky notes, then simply create three large areas side by side where you can write, draw, and place other normal-sized sticky notes. If you're doing this virtually, create three boxes on your digital whiteboard that you can fill in with other content. Label each area "current state," "in-between," and "transformation."

Write the Big Idea

Write your Big Idea down on an index card and place/tape it above your current state and transformation so you can see it easily. Think about how you will prove the Big Idea through the Transformation Tale you'll create.

Brainstorm the Current State

In the area labeled "Current State," brainstorm everything you can think of about the hero's current state. Use bullet points, scribble everywhere, draw a picture. Write down everything you can think of! These questions can be helpful starting places:

- *What does the hero (you, someone else, or the reader) want?*
- *What gets in the way of them getting what they want?*
- *What catalyst is disrupting their life?*
- *Why are they having that problem?*
- *How does that problem make them feel?*
- *How do they deny the situation or make it worse?*
- *What does it cost them?*

Brainstorm the Transformation

Write down everything you can think of about how the hero's life will be different by the end of the book. Ask yourself:

- *What will the hero know/think/do differently by the end of the book?*
- *What happens as a result of this transformation?*
- *For memoir, how does the internal journey resolve positively? Does the external journey resolve positively, negatively, or not at all?*

If you're tracking with us, then you'll probably realize we left something out: the in-between. How will the hero actually bridge the gap between where they are at the beginning of the book and the incredible transformation waiting for them at the end? Don't worry, we didn't forget.

Keep reading; the fun is just starting.

7

Outline Your Book Structure

Now that you have the bookends of your Transformation Tale, we've got to figure out how to fill the in-between. What guides the reader from the current state to the transformation? What mechanisms, stories, and principles get them from here to there? If you have the beginning and the ending of your manuscript, what's in the middle? Essentially, what actually *goes* in your book?

First, we're going to get all of your ideas on the page. Next, we're also going to organize your thoughts in a way that makes sense for your reader. You have to decide what comes first and last, which comes after which and why. There is a method to the madness of creating a cohesive manuscript, and it's called Book Structure.

Think about a body part—let's say your arm. Most days, you hardly think about your arms, but they're doing a lot of work, right? You only notice them when something's off. Maybe one of them is sore or you have a cut or perhaps, if you're really unlucky, you broke it. When that happens, you become acutely aware of your arm because it hurts, and it's making everything harder. That's how book structure works. Well-structured books have a hidden, secret matrix behind them that, when done well, casual readers won't even notice. They flow and help our brains digest the information. In narrative-driven books, they leave readers wanting more, and excited to get to the next chapter to see what happens. In prescriptive books, the knowledge or process you are teaching builds systematically in a way that your audience can learn and apply it flawlessly. Just like your arm when it's healthy and functioning—you hardly notice it.

But when book structure is off and doesn't work for the material you're trying to deliver, readers can tell. They might not even know why, but they can tell something is "off." Things don't click the way they are supposed to and, worst of all, your book doesn't impact them the way it could. "Book structure" might not be the sexiest two words ever put together, but believe us, this is the silent superhero (or villain) of your book. And, this is what can make you look like a true pro, even if you're not. Let's dig into how.

The Brain Dump

It's time to decide what goes between the introduction and conclusion of your book. It begins with a good ole brain dump. With your Transformation Tale in mind, the process of finding your chapters begins by noting or bulleting everything you know about what you want to say. Don't worry about what order it will go in, or if it's even worthy of inclusion right now. In the beginning, this is a judgment-free zone. The judgment comes later when we organize and analyze. Assume that if an idea pops into your head during this process, there's something to it. For now, just write. Here are some ways to think about this.

Think in Scenes

If your book follows a narrative of any kind, thinking in scenes can be a great way to start. If your life (or the life of your main character/protagonist) was a movie, what are the pivotal scenes? Start listing these in the in-between section in your Transformation Tale. You don't even have to go in chronological order. You can start with the climax. Does your memoir center around a traumatic loss? Or meeting someone in particular? Even if you're writing a prescriptive book that teaches a process, we bet there have been pivotal moments in your own story that shaped what you learned. Maybe there was a lightbulb moment during a conversation with a client. Maybe there was a huge failure that set you down a different path. What are the major scenes of your own movie that have to be included in your book?

Do not only focus on how potentially cinematic they are. Yes, a car crash might be an obvious, critical moment that must be included. But everyone's life stories are different and we all make meaning in unique ways. A random phone call on a Tuesday with a friend where she said the exact right thing and changed your life might be just as transformative. I (Liz) still think about a DM I got years ago on Instagram from someone I hardly know that included amazing advice for how to handle a hard time. It changed how I treat myself forever. One of my ghostwriting memoir clients experienced sexual trauma, so much of our outlining of her book understandably centered on that. But once we got into the nitty gritty of telling her story, she elaborated on a moment of reflection she had about her stepdad while pumping gas in the middle of nowhere. It turned out to be critical to the story and her (and the reader's) transformation. Your scenes are your scenes—big and small. Think them through carefully.

This is often the place to begin because there is so much the narrative of your own life can reveal about what it is you want to say. Even with my thought-leader, Big Idea writers, sometimes it's most helpful to start with their own life or life experience (even if it's professional) because the lessons we learn are revealed through stories and what happened to us. For a great resource on this, check out Donald Miller's book *Hero on a Mission: A Path to Meaningful Life*.

Think in Stories

In addition to thinking through the scenes of your own life, think about what other stories you want to include in your book. Maybe there are stories that illustrate a particular concept or piece of the process exceptionally well. You probably have stories of clients that you just know have to be told. For us, we knew from the very beginning of writing this book that we had to include the story of Brittany, as she is emblematic of everything we teach. Plus, she was the first client who proved to me that this can work for anyone. There are likely stories of the lives of others that you'd like to include. Write them down as well.

There's a good chance there are also examples in popular culture or history that come to mind. Don't forget about those in your brain dump. One of my clients had been incredibly impacted by Oprah over the years, both personally and professionally. We knew we had to include some enlightening and relevant stories about Oprah in her book to illustrate concepts. They meant a lot to the author and had the benefit of being a cultural touchpoint for readers. What client, friend, family, cultural, or historical stories do you want to include somehow in your book?

Think in Principles and Ideas

Of course, stories are not the only items you want to brain dump. Think through what ideas and principles you also want to communicate. Some early examples of the brain dump for this book included "book proposals," "mapping," and "comp titles." Some ideas went on to be chapters, some entire parts, and some just ideas within a chapter. Feel free to write down one word or a paragraph or two about themes and truths you want to expand on in your book.

Think in Action Steps

This primarily applies to our prescriptive nonfiction writers. Jot down what you want your reader to *do*. Are there imperative processes that must be included? Parts of a puzzle that are critical to success? Make sure you include those in your brain dump. When you walked through the Transformation Tale in your own life, what steps did you take, whether consciously or subconsciously? This book you are reading is a prescriptive book. We're teaching you a process—walking you through something you didn't know how to do before, and now you will. There are action steps attached. Are there similar parts to your book? What are you going to teach your reader? What wisdom do you have to impart? Brainstorm those in this process.

Think in Whatever You Want

Again, there are no rules here. We love a plan, and the only plan in this step is to make a mess. Write down quotes, descriptions, names of other books, or even random thoughts that you had in the middle of the night. You might need to set aside hours or even days for this process. Pour some coffee, light a candle, put on a little writing music, and let your creative juices flow.

Tips and Tricks:

1. If you're really blocked and having trouble brain dumping, try speaking out loud and recording yourself.
2. Another idea if you're having trouble is to do this with a trusted friend. Have them ask you questions about your book and topic to get things moving.
3. As the thoughts flow, feel free to follow a rabbit trail or zoom in on one topic at a time. This might be an easier way to get started if brain dumping about your whole book sounds intimidating.

Organize the Mess by Applying Logic

Alright, you should have a big, beautiful mess of a bunch of stuff you want to write about in the in-between column, or in your middle large sticky note. Ideas that will take your reader all the way from their current state to their desired transformation.

First, take a metaphorical (or literal) step back and look at your brain dump. Does anything instantly stand out to you? It's okay if not, but examine it just to see. Is there a clear order to the ideas? A picture emerging? Something that must go first and something that must go last? Maybe some parts begin to appear. Maybe you notice some groupings of ideas and stories that are similar and clearly go together. Are there larger ideas and smaller ideas? Maybe you even begin to notice some holes you need to fill or stories you've already decided to eliminate. Whatever comes up is totally fine. Let all of that marinate as we begin to organize.

Before we jump straight into a book structure, we want to identify any underlying logic patterns at play so that we can pick the best, most intuitive structure.

Let's take a look at a few ways to think about all of the material you're working with.

1. **Big to small.** As you start to organize your thoughts, maybe you notice that some of your ideas go from big to small. You could start with an overarching theme, like love, and move to the more granular ideas like different kinds of love or ways we express it. Like romance, family, friendships, or pets.
2. **Small to big.** Maybe you go in the reverse order and your book starts zoomed in and zooms back out. You could start with a story about love in one person's life and gradually zoom out to all humanity.
3. **Abstract to practical/concrete.** This is a common thing to notice, both in your brain dump and in published books. You could start with a high-level concept and move into the ways to apply it practically. If we take the theme of love again, perhaps your book explores the idea of what love is in the beginning and then moves into ways to show love, like the five love languages. The braindump for this book went about this way. In the beginning, we had ideas about helping writers get their work into the world, and then we moved into applicable tips like outlining and book proposals.
4. **Problem to solution.** This is another popular one for prescriptive books. This could look as simple as a two-part framework where you present the problem, and then show your reader the solution. Like "why you can't find love" and "here's how." Don't overcomplicate this. Sometimes the easiest option is the best one.
5. **Personal to global.** Maybe your Big Idea starts with your own journey and moves into how it applies to others, or even humanity at large. Similar to moving from small to big (or vice versa), you could start zoomed in on your own life and move into how those concepts apply to the world.

6. **Global to personal**. Okay, you get it. You can do this one in reverse, too.

7. **Order or process-specific**. Sometimes whatever you are teaching has an obvious process to it. If that's true for you, awesome! You won't have to struggle too much to find your book structure. Certain elements need to come before others. This is true for many industry experts who write a book about their expertise (like this one!). If you already have a course, class, or work with clients about your book subject matter, there's a good chance you already have a strong process. This doesn't always mean you won't struggle along the way deciding the order of things. But it is a great foundation and place to start.

A word of creative caution here. This is a messy, fluid, ongoing process. Never once in my professional life have I written and sold a book proposal that ended up with the exact number of chapters and parts in the same order with the same titles that the eventual book had. But you have to start somewhere. And so we start here. Know that this will change, and it's supposed to. You're not doing anything wrong if this doesn't feel exactly right yet. Continue to refine it as you map your book and even as you write it!

Common Structures for Prescriptive Books

With your brain dump in hand and a sprinkle of logic, let's talk through some common structures and see which best fits with your book idea. We'll start with prescriptive.

Sequential Approach

The sequential approach is great for all kinds of books, especially those that teach a specific process to move the reader from their current state to the transformation. It basically goes: you do this, then this, then this. Every piece of the process adds onto another, and the parts must be taught in that order, as you can see in figure 7.1. This book uses the sequential approach. You must determine your Big Idea before you can map out your book, write it, or thoughtfully consider your publishing options. Technically, you could do these things out of order, but it'd be tough and isn't advisable.

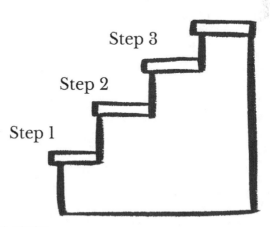

Figure 7.1. Sequential Book Structure

A great example of a sequentially structured book is Greg McKeown's bestseller, *Essentialism*.[1] His book is organized into four parts: Essence, Explore, Eliminate, and Execute, and there are chapters within each. These parts are meant to be implemented in order. You aren't supposed to execute before you eliminate what is not essential. Another example is *The 7 Habits of Highly Effective People*.[2] You might think that Stephen Covey's book is simply a list and explanation of the seven habits, and much of the book is. But all of the habits build on each other. You are meant to master habit 1 before habit 7. I certainly can't speak to Covey's process, but it's clear based on the structure and the writing that the concept of these habits building on one another was critical.

If you are struggling to articulate a process or a framework, asking yourself where *you* started when you walked through this transformation can be helpful. How did you go about solving the problem? No matter what genre you're writing in, if you have any personal connection to the material, it can be helpful to start with your own story. Even if you're writing a prescriptive book that teaches a process, it can still be based around your own narrative or the narrative of someone who exemplifies the process. Or, if you believe there is a process hidden somewhere in your material, but you're having trouble locating it, examining a story can often help you articulate it. Michael Singer's book *The Surrender Experiment* does a version of this.[3] Admittedly, this book blurs the lines of memoir and self-help. It's one of those mash-ups we mentioned earlier: a "teaching memoir." It follows Singer's story of a deep spiritual awakening and decision to let life unfold as it will, and has helpful takeaways and practical wisdom for the reader to implement in their own lives. And it's all organized entirely around Singer's incredible personal journey.

Do you see a sequential approach anywhere in your brain dump of ideas? Is there a method hidden in the madness? Are there parts that your reader must implement before others for the rest of what you teach to work at all? Make note of that and keep reading.

Pie Approach

In contrast to the previous structure, with the pie approach, the order of your chapters does not matter as much, or perhaps at all. When you're eating a real-life apple pie, it doesn't matter which piece you pick, right? That doesn't make the previous or subsequent slices any better or worse. You just grab whatever slice you want and it's awesome. Maybe your Big Idea is comprised of multiple smaller ideas that all contribute to the whole, but don't build upon each other, as shown in figure 7.2. You could pick one out at random and not be completely lost without the context of the rest of the book. Of course, all authors hope that readers will read their book start to finish. And most books are best read that way. But in a pie structure, fundamental concepts aren't introduced in chapter 1 that prevent ideas in chapter 7 from being applicable.

One popular example of this is Rachel Hollis's *Girl, Wash Your Face*.[4] In each chapter, she takes a common "lie" that women believe and debunks it. You could jump to chapter 9, "The Lie: I'm Not a Good Mom," and absorb the information just fine. Each individual lie contributes to the overall concept of the book that women are meant to lead fulfilling lives and not get down about the falsehoods that hold us back. Another best-selling book, Jen Sincero's *You Are a Badass*, does

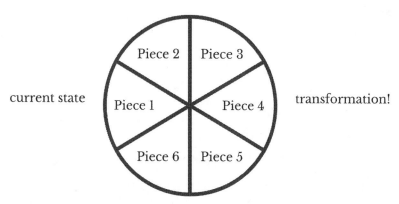

current state   transformation!

Figure 7.2. Pie Book Structure

something similar.[5] Each chapter covers one principle about how to achieve the financial, relational, and personal happiness you've been searching for.

Add Parts within Books

Here's where things get a little crazy (in a good way!). You can mix and match these structures by adding "parts," or overall sections, to further organize your book. Maybe your book is broken down into three parts, and each part has five chapters. Perhaps those three parts need to go in order. Part I has to go first and part III has to come last because they build on each other, so you implement a sequential order. But within those three parts, the order of each of the five chapters doesn't matter. Our book has four sequential parts. McKeown also does this in *Essentialism*. Earlier we said that he uses the sequential format for his book. But he also uses the pie method. Twist! Each of the five parts of the book has multiple chapters, and the order of those chapters within the parts doesn't matter.

Donald Miller's book *Marketing Made Simple* uses an even simpler format.[6] That book has only two parts. Part I has three chapters and part II has seven. (Quick note to say here that your parts don't even have to be balanced! The "right" amount of chapters is just however many is necessary. Sometimes there's simply less to say about a topic and that's perfectly fine.) Part I lays out the necessary foundational information and part II is the process for implementing the marketing plan. Part I needs to come first, but within part I, those three chapters use the pie approach. Then, within part II, we see another sequential structure, as the process needs to be implemented in order.

Our running example of *Atomic Habits* mixes formats, too.[7] Let's look at the table of contents:

Clear mixes the sequential and pie approaches. "The Fundamentals" and "Advanced Tactics" have to come first and last. But all the four laws, and the chapters within them, could go in any order. They do not build upon one another.

You can use all these approaches in as many ways as you'd like within your book. Again, there are no rules, which can feel both liberating and scary. Use these structures to put some guardrails around how you format your book and trust that these will help deliver the information in the best way for your reader.

Common Structures for Creative Nonfiction Books

Now let's take a look at creative nonfiction structures.

The Quest

The quest follows the classic hero's journey. Think Jason and his search for the golden fleece, Dorothy on the way to the Emerald City, Frodo journeying to the Undying Lands. It begins with a clear, inciting incident that sends our hero (you, if you're writing memoir) on a journey to seek a new life. Like your Transformation Tale, this journey could be either internal or external, and sometimes it's both. In Kate Bowler's memoir, *Everything Happens for a Reason, and Other Lies I've Loved*, she is diagnosed with cancer and goes on an internal journey to become at peace with this information and reexamine her beliefs about life and death. In *Eat, Pray, Love*, Gilbert divorces her husband, has an existential crisis, and actually leaves home and the familiar behind in search of a new life. First-timers and most narrative nonfiction writers, this is a great structure to start with. When it comes to storytelling, it's always a good idea to just start at the beginning.

The Rumble, the Reckoning, the Revolution

Brené Brown's book *Rising Strong* (a prescriptive nonfiction book!) has a subtitle that perfectly summarizes the three-part structure: the Reckoning, the Rumble, the Revolution. We give her all the credit and think it works great for any kind of story-based book. No surprise, Brown writes that she was inspired by Joseph Campbell for this story structure as well. In her book, Brown uses this formula to help readers "rise from our falls, overcome our mistakes, and face hurt in a way that brings more wisdom and wholeheartedness."[8]

It works like this. In the Reckoning, your protagonist becomes aware of their problem or obstacle. Something happens to them, an inciting incident of some kind. Like most things in creative nonfiction, this could be internal or external. It could be a car crash. It could be a realization. In the Rumble, things get rocky. Your protagonist struggles with this new situation and goes through the process of working through it. Often, things get worse before they get better. They try things that don't work, try on new identities, and seek new information. They are challenged and transformed along the way. Then comes the Reckoning, where the main character metaphorically rises from the ashes and into their transformation. They have learned something, they are forever changed, and they are living a new life.

Glennon Doyle's book *Untamed* is structured like this.[9] In part I, "Caged," Glennon tells the story of how she looked across the room while speaking at a conference one day and instantly fell in love with another woman—star soccer player, Abby Wambach. The only problem was, Glennon was married to a man. This begins her Rumbling with just about everything in her life—what it means to be a woman, a mother, a daughter, a partner—in part II, "Keys." She struggles with her sexual identity and what society has conditioned her to believe about herself. In part III, "Free," Glennon learns to listen to her own voice, the one who said from deep within when she first saw Abby, "There she is." She decides to stop abandoning herself and start living life on her own terms. Total Revolution.

Perhaps your story fits into a three-part structure like this as well. Note that the three parts do not have to be of equal length. Often the Reckoning (part I) is shorter and the Rumbling (part II)—where most of the learning happens—is the longest. If you are writing a story about overcoming, there's a good chance this structure will work well for your book.

Essay Structure

This structure looks like a collection of essays, usually one essay for each chapter or scene. It's best used for stories that focus on the internal journey rather than an external one and allows the author to be looser with timelines. Many of them skip around in time and don't pick up where the previous chapter left off. Emily Ratajkowski's beautiful memoir *My Body* is a great example. Each essay tells a story from Ratajkowski's life, some from childhood, and some from her days as one of the most famous and highest paid models in the world. She explores feminism, sexuality, power, beauty, and the commoditization of women, not through telling her story start to finish, but zeroing in on one experience at a time and dissecting what it meant for her life, and thus the reader's.

Dani Shapiro does something similar in her memoir *Inheritance*. After discovering through a genealogy test that her deceased father was not her biological father, Shapiro is sent on a journey of identity and what it means to belong. She jumps around in the timeline from past to present, taking readers on an investigative and poignant journey. If you have deep themes to explore and are interested in experimenting with more creative structures, writing in essays convened around one central Big Idea might be the way to go.

Experiment Structure

This type of book spans a specific period of time (usually fairly short, like a year) and centers on a specific challenge the author takes on or experiment they conduct. Often they blog or catalog their thoughts and findings along the way, sometimes with their audience in real-time. Some popular examples are Julie Powell's *Julia and Julia* (also turned into a Nora Ephron movie) in which she cooks her way through Julia Child's cookbook in a matter of months and blogs about it. Author Gretchen Rubin had already published two books but wasn't a household name until she wondered on a bus one day, "What *does* actually make people happy?" which led to her year-long experiment with happiness theories, and of course, her subsequent bestseller *The Happiness Project*.

An example lesser known but no less deserving of praise is Rachel Bertsche's *MWF Seeking BFF.* Newly married and living in a new city, Rachel sets out to make friends (and maybe find her BFF!) by going on one friend date a week for a year. She tells all manner of hilarious, fun, sad, and poignant stories in memoir as she recounts the honest struggle of making friends as an adult. You could even argue that *Eat, Pray, Love* fits into this structure, too, since Gilbert sets out on a year-long journey with the goal of finding herself again. We believe it better represents a quest so we listed it above, but you can see how these structures sometimes blend. Art is subjective and you can play and even cross-pollinate these.

The experiment structure is helpful because, as far as creative nonfiction goes, there are clearer parameters and goals than some other types of story-focused structures. If there is a concept or idea you've been mulling over, perhaps a question you want to answer, try experimenting with it for a set period of time. Bonus points if you report your findings in real-time to your audience. You might just land on an awesome book idea and find readers at the same time.

Decide on a Structure to Start

This process of outlining your book structure is the messy, hands-dirty, experimental part. It can be fun, frustrating, exciting, exhausting, and overwhelming. If you've felt any of that, you're completely normal. This might come quickly to you, or it might take time. You'll likely revise it more than once and then actually get into the writing process and revise your structure again in one way or another. It's common to get deep into the writing and realize what you thought was just a bullet point needs to be its own chapter. But in order to begin the writing at all, you must complete this important part of the mapping process. So go ahead, brain dump and organize what you come up with in the way that makes the most sense. And leave room to change things up as you move along in the creative process.

8

Plan Your Chapter

Prescriptive Nonfiction

Have you ever looked at a word that you've seen a thousand times and thought it suddenly looked weird? This is often what happens with aspiring authors when we try to plan out a chapter. We've seen them in other books a thousand times. Everyone knows what a chapter is, right?! But for some reason, when you sit down to write one for yourself, you suddenly have *no idea* what makes a chapter.

In this one, we'll help you get past this common stumbling block, particularly in prescriptive nonfiction books. A chapter about chapters—so meta, right? Mapping your chapter for creative nonfiction books (memoirs and narrative nonfiction) will be the focus of chapter 9. If you're writing creative nonfiction, feel free to skip ahead over there instead!

What Makes a Chapter?

Planning one individual chapter is a lot like planning the book itself, in miniature. Every chapter has its own little Big Idea, a "little transformation," and some key ideas that need to be organized, as you learned in chapter 7 for the whole book. So the answer to what makes a chapter is this: Every chapter has to achieve its own, smaller transformation for the hero of the book. When that little transformation is achieved, the chapter is done! The sequence of all of those chapters in a row creates a series of small transformations that culminates in the larger transformation of the entire book, like you saw in chapter 7.

The good news is: you already know how to do this! You're going to take the same principles you learned in the previous two chapters and apply them at a smaller scale to each chapter in your book, one at a time.

Decide Your Little Big Idea

Just as you did with your book's Big Idea, you'll need to articulate a "little" Big Idea for your chapter as well. This little Big Idea should be stated as a complete sentence, an argument; it's what you'll need to prove in your chapter.

For example, here are a few good little Big Ideas for chapters, from some prescriptive books:

- "Your habits change depending on the room you are in and the cues in front of you." —chapter 6, "Motivation Is Overrated; Environment Often Matters More," in *Atomic Habits* by James Clear[1]
- "Five decades into the war on cancer, it seems clear that no single 'cure' is likely to be forthcoming. Rather, our best hope likely lies in figuring out better ways to attack cancer on all three of these fronts: prevention, more targeted and effective treatments, and comprehensive and accurate early detection." —chapter 8, "The Runaway Cell," in *Outlive* by Peter Attia[2]
- "We own our stories so we don't spend our lives being defined by them or denying them." —chapter 3, "Owning Our Stories," in *Rising Strong* by Brené Brown[3]

Notice that all of these little Big Ideas are quotes from the pages of these chapters themselves; the authors don't keep the little Big Idea hidden from the reader. Look them up, and I challenge you to look for little Big Ideas stated succinctly in each chapter of the prescriptive books you have on your shelves. The little Big Idea summarizes the argument that chapter is making and often gives a preview of the key points that will be discussed. The argument is then proven explicitly through the key points, exercises, illustrations, and other elements in the chapter.

Q&A

Q: How do I know that my little Big Idea isn't too small or too big?
A: Getting the scope right is tough! We find that most authors tend to err on the side of making their little Big Ideas *too* big. The just-right size for your little Big Idea is that it's the smallest single component that you can prove. If you find yourself trying to prove multiple pieces of an idea, then your little Big Idea is probably too big and might need to be divided into multiple chapters.

Make Your Chapter's Little Transformation Tale

Now that you know what you're trying to prove in a chapter, we recommend creating a "little Transformation Tale" to get clear on where this chapter will start and where it will end—the current state and the transformation. Let's continue on with chapter 6 of *Atomic Habits*.

Notice that your chapter's little Transformation Tale will be smaller than the Transformation Tale for the entire book—as it should be. In fact, you should be able to summarize the Transformation Tale for one chapter in just a few words or phrases.

Table 8.1. Example Little Transformation Tale: Chapter 6, "Motivation Is Overrated; Environment Often Matters More" in *Atomic Habits* by James Clear

Current State	In-Between	Transformation
• Reader believes that motivation is the key to forming new habits • Unaware of how influenced they are by their environment • Unsure how to set themselves up for success with new habits		• Understands that environment shapes habits • Knows how to curate their environment for the habits they want to adopt

Think about what the reader is moving *from* and going *to*. For example, we could summarize the Transformation Tale for chapter 6 in *Atomic Habits* as: "from motivation to environment." Obviously, there's a lot more to unpack there (hence the need for an entire chapter devoted to this!), but we know it's a strong idea because it can be boiled down fairly simply.

What Goes in Each Chapter?

Just as we planned the in-between for the whole book—all the content that will create the transformation—we need to plan the in-between for each chapter as well. How will you lead the reader to that little transformation in the space of a few thousand words? And how will you keep the reader interested and engaged the whole way through? Chapter lengths for prescriptive nonfiction books typically range between 2,500–6,000 words. This is much longer than the average blog post (700–2,000 words), and many first-time authors haven't written something this long since they were in school!

We find that many authors can get through the planning of their Transformation Tales and book structure—but when they get to the chapters, the place where the real thinking and writing needs to happen, they feel completely unprepared and get flustered. To get past the terror of the blank page, they start to word vomit on the topic they've chosen for that chapter. What comes out is wandery, full of tangents, and disorganized. They know it, too. We hear these authors say things like, "I don't know what I'm trying to say anymore," or "I'm afraid this is boring."

We want to help you approach each chapter with confidence and clarity, so that you know exactly what to write and how you're going to prove your little Big Idea while keeping the reader engaged.

A Note on Entertainment vs. Engagement

Your job as a prescriptive nonfiction author is not to entertain your reader. Yup, that's right! Your job is, rather, to *engage* the reader. Entertainment is mindless consumption; it doesn't require any mental effort or energy on the part of the reader. Engagement, on the other hand, asks the reader to become an active participant in the content. When you engage the reader, they can't help but think about the argument you're making, even after they put the book down to go wash the dishes or put the kids to bed. They wrestle with the story in their minds; they weigh it against their own experience. They come up with counterpoints and ask questions. *That* is what gets the reader to come back to your book again and again. *That* is what gets the reader to hand it to their friend and say, "You have to read this." Readers love to be engaged.

Prescriptive nonfiction chapters have a fairly standard set of elements that you can use to engage the reader and build your case. You saw these elements at the beginning of part II. Here they are again in figure 8.1:

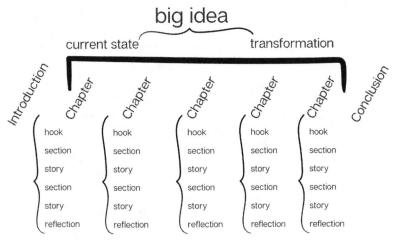

Figure 8.1. Sample Prescriptive Nonfiction Book Map

We'll go through them one by one—as well as some additional elements not listed here!

Hooks

Every chapter should start with a hook, an enticement designed to make your reader curious about the chapter. But hooks don't just stop there; great hooks go one step further by leading the reader to your little Big Idea for the chapter. They create a trail of breadcrumbs, ending with an explicit statement of the little Big Idea. But what does that trail of breadcrumbs look like?

Interesting Story

The most popular way to hook a reader is to tell a story. But it can't just be any story; if you're going to use a story at the beginning of the chapter, it should illustrate the little Big Idea. Let's take a look at one of our favorite examples.

In Dan Pink's book *To Sell Is Human*, the little Big Idea for chapter 1 is stated succinctly in the chapter's title: "We're All in Sales Now." That's the argument Pink is making in this very first chapter. So he needs a story that will help lead the reader to that argument—and he has one. Here are the first two sentences of the chapter:

> Norman Hall shouldn't exist. But here he is—flesh, blood, and bow tie—on a Tuesday afternoon, sitting in a downtown San Francisco law office explaining to two attorneys why they could really use a few things to spruce up their place.[4]

Pink zeroes in on an interaction between Norman Hall and these lawyers, where Hall successfully entices the lawyers to buy some cleaning supplies. The hook ends with (spoiler alert) the reveal that Norman is the very last door-to-door salesman for the Fuller Brush Company.

Besides that delightfully surprising opening, this hook works well for a couple reasons:

- Pink is reminding us of a bygone era, not just explicitly but also hinted at in details like Norman Hall's bow tie.
- He's getting us to think about how many door-to-door salesmen we still see these days. The answer? Not many. In fact, not *any*.

The punchline of this hook is that door-to-door salesmen like Norman don't exist anymore. Why not? It's not because businesses don't need to sell anymore. Rather, it's because (and this is the little Big Idea of this chapter) *all of us are salespeople now.*

That's how a great story hook works, leading the reader along a logical path to the argument the author is making.

Compelling Question

Another way to engage the reader at the beginning of the chapter is to ask a compelling question. Again, not just any question will do; it has to be a question related to the little Big Idea. Here's how personal finance guru Ramit Sethi does it in chapter 6, "The Myth of Financial Expertise" in his book *I Will Teach You to Be Rich*: "If I invited you to a blind taste test of a $12 wine versus a $1,200 wine, could you tell the difference?"[5]

At first blush, you might not see the connection to the little Big Idea. Is this chapter about wine? But stick with it for a minute. This question immediately gets the reader thinking about their own level of expertise and how we acquire knowledge in specific areas. The average reader would probably answer this question by thinking, "There's no way I could tell the difference; I'm not an expert!" That's exactly what Sethi wants you to think.

Sethi goes on to share about an experiment where expert sommeliers were invited to taste test two different wines and compare them. Shockingly, the wine experts failed the experiment! His point is: Experts don't always know what they're talking about—including financial experts. This is the little Big Idea he sets out to prove in this chapter.

In this case, Sethi's technique is actually a bit of a feint; he is leading the reader down the *wrong* logical path on purpose, so that he could make a bigger impression with the big reveal in the story of the wine experts. It's engaging because it surprises us.

Your question hook doesn't have to similarly surprise or mislead the reader; it could be more straightforward. Either way, you have to use the question to lead the reader to that little Big Idea.

Surprising Data/Statement

Another way to hook the reader is to come right out and hit them with something surprising. Robin Diangelo accomplishes this feat in chapter 2, "Racism and White Supremacy," of her wave-making book *White Fragility*:

> Many of us have been taught to believe that there are distinct biological and genetic differences between races.[6]

Her readers (intended to be white Americans) are likely thinking, *Yup, that's true* . . .

A few sentences later, she hits us with this bold statement:

> Under the skin, there is no true biological race. The external characteristics that we use to define race are unreliable indicators of genetic variation between any two people.

BOOM. That's not what her reader was expecting! It's a surprising argument that Diangelo goes on to prove in the chapter.

This is a technique that our friend Jeff Goins likes to teach aspiring authors, as we mentioned in chapter 5. He shares a formula that goes like this: *Everybody thinks X, but the truth is Y.*

To use this technique, first state something that most people generally tend to agree with (but you secretly disagree with). Then reveal "the truth" that goes against that assumption—just like Diangelo did. After that, you'll need to back up your statement with evidence, but you've successfully caught your reader's attention! This is one of our favorite hook techniques.

Analogy

The last type of hook that you might consider using for your chapter is to make an analogy—that is, an interesting comparison between your topic and another topic that can illustrate your little Big Idea. Ramit Sethi did this with the wine experts in our question example above. The writer Verlyn Klinkenborg also does this in his book *Several Short Sentences About Writing*:

> This is a book of first steps. Their meaning will change as your experience changes. This book contains the bones of many arguments and observations—a vertebrae here, a mandible there—but the whole skeleton is what you make of it.[7]

Klinkenborg wants the reader to focus on the bare essentials of their writing, just one individual sentence at a time. The analogy of bones provides a helpful way of describing the focus he wants the reader to maintain on just the "bones" of their ideas.

Q&A

Q: Can I mix and match hooks?
A: Absolutely, yes! You've already seen this in a couple of the examples we've shared so far. Many books use a story to introduce a compelling question, which leads us to the little Big Idea. Or they offer an analogy and end with a surprising kicker. These hook techniques often work well in tandem with each other.

Q: How long should hooks be?
A: Hooks can vary in length, depending on what type of hook you use. Stories will likely be a little longer, maybe up to a page or two, while surprising statements or questions could be a single sentence!

Whatever type of hook you decide to use, don't forget to state your little Big Idea explicitly at the end. Don't keep it hidden from the reader! Tell them exactly what you want to prove to them in this chapter. Then you can dive right into your key ideas.

Key Points

You'll need two to five points throughout your chapter to help make your case. We recommend using these points as subheadings throughout the chapter to break up the text, help the reader transition to new ideas, and remind the reader of the progress they're making toward that chapter's little transformation.

But what should these key ideas be? The answer will depend on whatever you're trying to prove in that chapter.

For example, in chapter 6 of *Atomic Habits*, there are a few key points that James Clear makes to back up his little Big Idea: "Your habits change depending on the room you are in and the cues in front of you." Here are the key points he makes in this chapter to help back up his argument and deliver the transformation for the reader (in his own words):

- "A small change in what you *see* can lead to a big shift in what you *do*."[8]
- "Every habit is initiated by a cue, and we are more likely to notice cues that stand out."[9]
- "Over time your habits become associated not with a single trigger but with the entire *context* surrounding the behavior."[10]

Clear consolidated these ideas into just two main sections of this chapter: "How to Design Your Environment for Success" and "The Context Is the Cue." Then, he backed up his claims with evidence, explanation, and research where appropriate.

Your key points are the areas where you get to fully explain your thinking, share your opinion, and make your case.

Stories

We already talked about using stories as hooks, but you may wish to use stories throughout your chapter as well. Stories can work either as cautionary tales or positive exemplars to illustrate your key points. These stories can come from your own personal experience (especially if your goal is to teach the reader how to overcome something you had to work through in your own life), from clients or customers, or even from historical figures or celebrities. You might also consider creating a fictional character to use in your prescriptive nonfiction book so that you can design the exact right circumstances and situation to help make your case. The point is: You can find stories all over the place! We'll talk more about *how* to find these stories in chapter 9 on mining for content.

In *Atomic Habits*, James Clear shares the story of how *Suggestion Impulse Buying* was conceived and tested (and is now ubiquitously used at stores) to put products in prominent places so that customers will spontaneously buy them.[11] This story supports his key point that "A small change in what you *see* can lead to a big shift in what you *do*."

Visuals

Visual elements can also be helpful for illustrating your key points, in the form of charts, graphs, tables, or images. The rule for visuals is that they should never be purely decorative; instead, visuals should enhance the reader's understanding of your key points throughout the chapter. Look at the way we've used visuals like figure 8.1 to help you understand chapter structure; hopefully, that visual brings to life the information in a deeper way! (Forgive us for using ourselves as an example; we're trying to practice what we preach. Plus, if we use ourselves as an example, we don't have to ask anybody else for permission. Double plus: It's our book. We can do what we want!)

Reader Interaction

Asking the reader to *do* something is a great way to engage them throughout your chapter. This gets readers not just taking in the knowledge you're telling them, but also helps them start to apply it in their lives. Again, this works particularly well for how-to books or books that are heavy on explicitly teaching the reader something. Reader interaction can take the form of templates, exercises, worksheets, trackers, and so on. If you want a sneak peek at some reader interaction, flip ahead to chapter 11 where we ask you to set your writing goals!

Closing and Transition

Wrapping up a chapter is often the hardest part. We recommend that your closing should include at least these three things:

- Revisit the hook, especially if that hook was a story. Go back to the beginning of the chapter and remind the reader of how you got them thinking.
- Restate your little Big Idea and the transformation the reader can achieve in this chapter.
- Transition to the next chapter. Tell the reader how what they learned in this chapter leads into the next chapter. How does what they've learned here prepare them for what's coming next?

It's also common to *end* chapters with some reader interaction, usually in the form of reflection questions or key takeaways. Key takeaways are a handy way to summarize your key points from the chapter to make them easier for readers to reference again. Reflection questions can also be a great way to encourage readers to discuss and apply what they've learned. This reader interaction is optional, but can be a fun and meaningful way to end a chapter. One important note, though: Be consistent! If you decide to end one chapter with key takeaways, add them to *all* of your chapters.

We can see these pieces at work in the closing of chapter 6 of *Atomic Habits* as well:

> If you can manage to stick with this strategy, each context will become associated with a particular habit and mode of thought. [RESTATING THE TRANSFORMATION]
>
> Habits thrive under predictable circumstances like these. Focus comes automatically when you are sitting at your work desk. Relaxation is easier when you are in a space designed for that purpose. Sleep comes quickly when it is the only thing that happens in your bedroom. [RECALLING THE HOOK]
>
> If you want behaviors that are stable and predictable, you need an environment that is stable and predictable. A stable environment where everything has a place and a purpose is an environment where habits can easily form.[12] [RESTATING THE LITTLE BIG IDEA]
>
> The chapter then ends with a "Chapter Summary" that includes a bulleted list of key takeaways for the reader. [READER INTERACTION]

Q&A

Q: How do you write great chapter titles?
A: Chapter titles should be derived from your chapter's little Big Idea. For prescriptive nonfiction books, we find that engaging chapter titles are either phrased as a directive to the reader (like the chapter titles in this book!), or they make an interesting argument ("We're All in Sales Now" or "Motivation Is Overrated; Environment Often Matters More").

Map It Out

Just as you have with Transformation Tales (chapter 6) and book structure (chapter 7), we recommend that you try mapping out a chapter from one of your comp books *before* you map out a chapter of your own so that you can see how other authors put all of these elements together to prove their little Big Idea.

If you're mapping a comp book chapter first, look for the chapter's little Big Idea (hint: it'll usually be right after the hook!) and write it down on an index card or sticky note. Place that at the top of your table, window, or area where you'll be working. If you're mapping out your own chapter, write down your little Big Idea here. Next, see if you can summarize this chapter's little transformation succinctly. We usually phrase this as the chapter moving the reader "from X to Y." Write that transformation on the back of your little Big Idea's index card.

Mapping out the in-between of your chapters is where things can get bright and colorful! If you're using sticky notes, then we recommend designating different colored stickies for hooks, stories within the chapter, key points, visuals, and reader interaction. If your index cards or sticky notes are all the same color, you can use different colored pens or Sharpies to get the same color-coding effect.

Then, take the time to think through every single element for your chapter. How can you engage the reader from the beginning? What key points do you want to include? What stories will you use from your own life or others' lives to illustrate those key points? Where would a chart or graph aid in the reader's understanding? How could you help the reader apply what they've learned with some reader interaction?

You can see how the elements you choose are going to look different for each chapter, depending on your little Big Idea. (That's why we focused on that first!) Whenever you feel stuck, return to your little Big Idea. Make sure you're clear on what you're trying to say—then the rest of the decisions become easier.

Don't rush this process. When we do this with clients, mapping each chapter can often take an hour or more! If you do that for all your chapters, it's often eight to ten hours total. It can be exhausting to do this much thinking and planning, so eat healthy meals, exercise, and take breaks. If you can do this in your own home, feel free to spread this process out over a few days so that you can come back to it regularly.

When it's all done, your map for just one chapter might look something like the one in figure 8.2 (again, for chapter 6 from *Atomic Habits*).

Every chapter will look a little different, and that's ok—but ideally all your chapters will follow some kind of consistent pattern. This is what makes your book feel purposeful and cohesive to the reader. Once you practice mapping out your chapters, you'll find a rhythm and it'll start to come more easily.

Little Big Idea	Chapter 6 Your habits change depending on the room you are in and the cues in front of you
Hook	"choice architecture" story
Key Point #1	design your environment for success
Story/Data	Dutch energy study
Personal Example	changing cues in my life
Key Point #2	the context is the cue
Sub-point	it's easier to change habits in new places
Personal Example	moving to a new house
Closing	chapter summary

Figure 8.2. Sample Chapter Map from Atomic Habits

Hopefully you have a pretty solid idea now of what actually goes into prescriptive nonfiction books and their chapters, and how you can plan your own. In chapter 9, we'll show you how this process works for creative nonfiction chapters—particularly for memoir and narrative nonfiction.

9

Plan Your Chapter

Creative Nonfiction

In creative nonfiction, we hold the idea of a "chapter" more loosely; here, a chapter is not so much a unit of ideas as it is a window on one piece of the story we want to tell. With prescriptive nonfiction, we take a more didactic approach to planning: we decide the topic and argument for the chapter, and then we fill in content to support that argument. With creative nonfiction, we often work backward: First, you decide what scenes and moments are important to include in the story; then you look for the structure that makes the most sense—which you did in chapter 7.

It sounds a bit mystical, and we confess, there is always a bit of mystery in the process of writing memoir and narrative nonfiction. That's because real life doesn't come neatly organized into a hierarchy of ideas and content; it is messy, it defies logic and reasoning. Yes, you need to have something to say, a Big Idea for your book—and you do, after chapter 3—but *how* you say it can take any number of forms. Trust your intuition to help you decide what is important and what is not necessary for the reader to know.

You already have an idea of the overall structure that will work for your book and a brain dump of all the important scenes and moments that need to be included. But how do you decide what pieces of the story will become your chapters? In this chapter, we want to help aspiring creative nonfiction writers plan out the chapters that will inspire and uplift your readers as you move toward the transformation.

Your Chapter's Little Transformation

In a creative nonfiction book, each chapter is one discrete piece of the whole transformation. It shows how your hero (you, if you're writing memoir) changes in one smaller, distinct way on their way to the overall transformation. So the first thing to do when looking for your chapters is to identify these smaller transformations. Look at your brain dump of scenes. Pick one or a few where something pretty significant changed for you. There's no exact right number of scenes or moments that should make up a chapter—one chapter might just have one important scene, or one chapter might have twenty small moments—what matters is that *something significant changes* in the internal journey. That change might be:

- From **bad** to **good** (positive internal transformation)
- From **good** to **bad** (negative internal transformation)
- From **bad** to **worse** (negative internal transformation)
- From **good** to **even better!** (positive internal transformation)

The Story Grid team calls this back-and-forth change the "polarity shift" of the scene.[1]

For example, in chapter 1 of *Eat, Pray, Love*, we find Elizabeth Gilbert walking back to her apartment in Italy with a tall, dark, and handsome man named Giovanni, who's been helping her learn Italian. She hopes that he'll kiss her goodnight and fantasizes about what that would be like—even though she also tells us she's trying to remain celibate while in Italy.

They get to the door, he gives her a hug, and then . . . nothing. Giovanni leaves and Liz says, "I am alone, I am all alone, I am completely alone."[2] If the chapter stopped there, we might say that this was a negative change for Liz—from *fantasy* (good) to *reality* (bad), or perhaps from *romantic possibility* (good) to *loneliness* (bad).

But that's not where it ends. Instead, after the door closes, Liz falls to her knees and says a prayer of gratitude. This moment is actually a tiny victory for Liz, revealing that this chapter's shift is actually positive—from *temptation* (bad) to *integrity* (good). Remember that Liz's internal invitation for the whole book is to discover who she is and remain true to herself. In this first chapter, we've seen her take one itty-bitty step toward that goal. (Note that the first chapter of *Eat, Pray, Love* begins with Elizabeth Gilbert already in Italy. This is a technique called *in medias res*—starting in the beginning of the action. This is a great way to hook your readers!)

Not every chapter can have a positive internal shift, though. In chapter 2, Liz Gilbert takes us back in time to the start of her inciting incident of the book. In this chapter, she's crying on the bathroom floor and finally admits that, despite trying for a baby with her husband, she really doesn't want a baby. And not only that; she doesn't want to be married anymore. This is the first piece of her external catalyst (getting divorced), which unfolds over the next few short chapters. The transformation here is from *pretending everything is fine* (bad, but stable) to *everything is definitely not fine* (worse).

This is a negative internal transformation; the chapter does *not* end on a high note, as the book will need to. That's because we're still working our way to the overall transformation of the book, and it's ok for individual chapters to end on a low note. In fact, in creative nonfiction books, each chapter—indeed, every scene—exists on a kind of seesaw of emotions, sometimes ending on a high note, and other times (often) ending on a low note.

Prescriptive nonfiction books don't have this emotional back and forth; in those books, every chapter ends on a high note as the reader learns one more component of what they need to achieve their overall transformation. Like climbing a ladder, each chapter takes the reader one step closer to the top.

We recommend brainstorming this series of transformations for every possible chapter. Yes, it's a lot of work! But by the end of it, you'll know *exactly* what needs to go in each chapter. Then, if there are transformations that happen over multiple chapters, you might want to add parts to the book as well, likely using the three-part structure inspired by Brené Brown (the Reckoning, the Rumble, and the Revolution) that we talked about in chapter 7.

Find the Little Big Idea

Within each little transformation, there's often also a broader lesson in this change that's applicable to all readers. This is the little Big Idea for that chapter. It's the golden nugget that readers will find and think to themselves, "Yes, I know that feeling, too!" These little Big Ideas are what make a memoir or narrative nonfiction—a very specific story—feel universal and relatable to wide swaths of readers.

Here are some little Big Ideas from creative nonfiction books:

- "How quickly victims must begin fighting, converting feelings into logic, navigating the legal system, the intrusion of strangers, the relentless judgment." —chapter 2 in *Know My Name* by Chanel Miller[3]
- "The more you invest in a set of beliefs—the greater the sacrifice you make in the service of that conviction—the more resistant you will be to evidence that suggests that you are mistaken. You don't give up. You double

down." —chapter 5, "General Hansell Was Aghast," in *The Bomber Mafia* by Malcolm Gladwell[4]

- "Right to die in America is about as meaningful as the right to eat or the right to decent housing; you've got the right, but it doesn't mean you're going to get the goods." —"Right to Die," *In Love: A Memoir of Love and Loss* by Amy Bloom[5]

Not every chapter has to have some kind of universal truth to it; the only requirement is that there's a little transformation. But if you can find one, all the better!

Inviting Your Readers In

So now that you know exactly how your hero changes throughout each chapter on the way to the overall transformation—how will you actually write out those important scenes or moments? We want to introduce you to two tools that will help you craft a compelling story and invite the reader to experience it with you: **zooming in** and **zooming out**.

You've probably heard the phrase, "Show, don't tell," when it comes to writing, right? That phrase has good intentions, but it's wrong. It should really be: "Show *and* tell." You need to both *show* the reader the important moments of your story (zoom in), and *tell* the reader the context they need to understand the significance of those moments (zoom out). Let's take a look at each of these tools.

Zooming In

Imagine your story like a movie. In the important scenes, we get to see the full dialogue and the emotional impact on the characters. We *zoom in* on the moments that we want the reader to remember. In fact, zooming in is a subtle sign to the reader to pay attention, because something important is happening. If you zoom in and something important *doesn't* happen, the reader will feel duped. This is a common mistake that memoir writers make, because to the author, every moment is important. We live our lives zoomed-in, feeling the full color and emotional impact of every second. But the reader can't bear all of that intensity; they won't be able to tell what's important from what's not. It's usually not until much later, once we've gained some perspective and distance, that we can say, "This period of time was, on the whole, not very important to the story I'm trying to tell." We have to use zooming in very carefully and strategically.

So what exactly does zooming in look like? It usually involves heavy dialogue and description, allowing the reader to experience the scene from the hero's point of view. This is a powerful empathic strategy that enables the reader to feel what you (if you're the hero) felt during this moment. Think of some of the most important moments in your life, the moments when you can still remember exactly what you were wearing, what you were doing, what the weather was like, and what was said when the IMPORTANT THING happened. The cliché of *time stood still* applies to these moments, because you must slow down the pace of the storytelling in order to capture every single little aspect of the scene. The vivid detail is itself a signal of how meaningful it was to you—and therefore, we need to use the same vivid details to tell the reader that this scene is important. This is zooming in.

Here's an example of how Elizabeth Gilbert does it in chapter 1:

> Now it is midnight and foggy, and Giovanni is walking me home to my apartment through these back streets of Rome, which meander organically around the ancient buildings like bayou streams snaking around shadowy clumps of cypress groves. Now we are at my door. We face each other.

He gives me a warm hug. This is an improvement; for the first few weeks, he would only shake my hand. I think if I were to stay in Italy for another three years, he might actually get up the juice to kiss me. On the other hand, he might just kiss me right now, tonight, right here by my door . . . there's still a chance . . . I mean we're pressed up against each other's bodies beneath this moonlight . . . and of course it would be a *terrible* mistake . . . but it's still such a wonderful possibility that he might actually do it right now . . . and that he might just bend down . . . and . . . and . . .[6]

This paragraph is so powerful because it feels as though you are *living* the experience with her. It's written in the present tense, so that we seem to be discovering the moment right along with Liz. Although you can show in either present or past tense, using the present tense is a clever way to draw the reader in deeper. Perhaps you can relate to the desire and longing you've felt when walking with a crush, hoping against hope that maybe they'll make a move—that breathless, desperate anxiety somewhere between hope and dread. Elizabeth Gilbert doesn't just tell us "I wish Giovanni would kiss me" (which is the first line of this chapter), she sweeps us up in her craving, making us read faster to see what will happen next.

These are the scenes where the reader will identify with us, where they'll feel that swelling sensation in their chest that says, *I know exactly what that feels like!* These are the scenes that will get us five-star reviews on Goodreads and Amazon, that will persuade the reader to give the book to a friend and say, "You have to read this!!"

And remember, not every single moment of your memoir or narrative nonfiction can be zoomed in. A constant, zoomed-in narrative would be exhausting. You have to balance it by zooming out.

Tips and Tricks for Zooming In

- Use strong, active verbs and avoid embellishing with adverbs ("she slurped hungrily," "he laughed maniacally")
- Use your five senses ("the wind was warm," "she was blinded by the headlights," "he smelled of cigars and pinewood")

Zooming Out

Zooming out is useful for conveying information that is essential for the reader to know, but not necessary for them to *experience*. It's best for setting the stage, conveying preexisting personality traits and character quirks, establishing context, and covering large expanses of time where things are relatively stable. Zooming out can also be a useful strategy for conveying feelings of lethargy and boredom (as long as you don't overdo it!).

Let's skip ahead to chapter 5, when Elizabeth Gilbert is navigating her divorce:

> Months passed. My life hung in limbo as I waited to be released, waited to see what the terms would be. We were living separately (he had moved into our Manhattan apartment), but nothing was resolved. Bills piled up, careers stalled, the house fell into ruin and my husband's silences were broken only by his occasional communications reminding me what a criminal jerk I was.[7]

In this paragraph, Gilbert is painting a picture. She's giving us a sense of what life was like in the aftermath of the divorce—but she doesn't want to drag us down into the depths of it with her. Instead, she describes the state of their crumbling marriage in more general terms: "Bills piled up, careers

Tips and Tricks for Zooming Out

- Use concrete references to large expanses of time ("six months later," "for the next five years," "the following September")
- Summarize the time and/or location ("During these years, Germany's military was substantially reduced")
- Use absolutes ("she always laughed at his jokes," "he never liked it when the teacher called on him")

stalled, the house fell into ruin. . . ." She's setting us up, preparing us for the coming zoom-ins when she'll get unstuck.

Sometimes it can be hard to tell the difference between zooming in (showing) and zooming out (telling). Sometimes authors still use vivid descriptions and imagery while zoomed out. Wouldn't that be showing? In this case, no—because the author is using those vivid details to tell us *what life is like*, to establish context and set our expectations for the status quo.

In some ways, writing chapters in creative nonfiction books is more straightforward: just tell the story! You'll find that often these chapters tend to go back and forth between zooming in and zooming out. Establish a little bit of context, and then bring the reader into an important moment. Rinse and repeat until the little transformation for that chapter has been accomplished.

Piece of cake, right?

Obviously, this is easier said than done. Sometimes, it can be hard to figure out how to fill the spaces in-between, even when we know what we want to say and what the transformation of our book should be. For that, you'll need to dig deep. In part III, we'll show you how to mine for content, set writing goals, establish productive writing rhythms, and then finally edit your masterpiece.

Onward!

Part III

WRITE YOUR DRAFT

Hey, hey, look at you! You have a whole freaking book mapped out in front of you. You did it! Now all you have to do is write it! Maybe you were so excited about finishing your book map and seeing the idea that only lived in your head for so long written out on the page that you've already started.

If so, you have probably already discovered what so many professional writers know: coming up with tens of thousands of words can be hard. But it is made much easier now that you have your book and chapters mapped out. You know the transformation that you're guiding your reader through and all of the little ideas along the way that you need to illustrate to get them there. Friends, that's half the battle.

The other half is the back half of this book: tap, tap, tapping away on the keyboard, day by day, until you have a complete manuscript. In part III, we'll explore where to come up with all the content that will fill your pages, how to hold yourself accountable and actually get the work done, what to do when you're stuck, and how to polish it when you're finished. Most of what we've covered so far has been about planning. Now it's all about execution. Get ready, authors, it's time to write a book.

10

Mine for Content

One of the coolest things about writing a book, or any writing project in general, is that you might begin to see ideas relevant to it all around you. You will probably experience the Baader-Meinhof phenomenon where your awareness of something increases, even though nothing has changed except your attention and perspective. Some people know this as the "red car phenomenon." This is when you start to notice how many red cars there are on the road because you've just bought one. "Wow, everyone went out and bought a red car!" you might think. When really, there's always been that many red cars; they've just never been relevant to you because you didn't own one.

The same may be true of your book. You'll find inspiration in the movies you're watching, books you're reading, and conversations you have every day. It's normal for our book ideas to bleed over into every area of our lives. But you will also get stuck sometimes. There will be times when you have to go looking for ideas to write about in order to fill chapters, so that's what we're covering here.

The process of writing your book begins with *thinking* about it. (*Duh*, right? But hold up. Maybe not so duh.) Here's a secret all authors eventually learn: good writing is just good thinking. And your brain needs space for that good thinking. Malcolm Gladwell said, "Writing is not the time-consuming part. It's knowing what to write. It's the thinking and the arranging and the interviewing and the researching and the organizing. That's what takes time. Writing is blissful. I wish I could do it more."[1] It's time to figure out what to write through good thinking.

Remember, for prescriptive nonfiction, you are going to need a mix of stories (likely from your own life and others' lives), compelling questions, data/statistics, analogies, visuals, action plans, and ideas of how to interpret these for your reader in order to create a compelling transformation. If you are writing creative nonfiction, especially memoir, you will mostly need stories from your own life or those of your subject, though you can find inspiration from and include other devices to enhance your work.

So how do you come up with all the components necessary to engage your reader and help them along the transformation to their final destination? You go on a mining expedition—a *content*-mining expedition. You'll have to do a little digging to unearth the gems hidden among the rough and sift through what's out there to figure out what deserves a place in your manuscript. Strap on your hard hats, everyone, we're going spelunking.

Brainstorm

So often in creative work, we start here, with a brainstorm. There's a good chance you already know more than you think you do if you just give yourself a little space to let the ideas flow. Like when we brain-dumped while we were looking for structure, withhold judgment when you brainstorm for what content to include in chapters as well. While looking at a specific chapter, here are some questions to ask yourself:

1. What does the reader/protagonist feel or know at this stage in the book?
2. What do they need to know/learn/understand to get them through the little transformation of this chapter?
3. Do the questions above recall stories from my own life where I've felt/experienced something similar?
4. Do any examples or data I've read about elsewhere come to mind?
5. Have I seen anyone in my personal or professional life experience the idea or process of this chapter?
6. What could I say or find that supports my argument?
7. Can I think of a fictitious example or analogy to illustrate a concept?
8. If I had the perfect story right here, what would it look like?

These are just a few questions to get you started. Put away distractions, silence your inner editor, and meditate on the thesis of each chapter before you begin mining for content elsewhere. If you are a chatty or more auditory-inclined person, it might help to do this with a friend, book coach, or even speak out loud and record yourself.

An important reason we recommend brainstorming first is because it can be helpful to let your own original ideas and thought process guide the research that comes next. All of these different kinds of content devices are meant to support what you have to say about your topic. So, start with what *you* know about it. Your brainstorm can even include questions you might need to research, because of course you won't know everything.

Get everything you know already on the page first. Now, examine the gaps. Do you need another story or two? Do you have a lot of your own opinion and not enough data to back it up? Do you need more references to well-known figures? Do you need a really great analogy? Awesome, let's go find them. These are some of the places you can mine.

Mine Your Personal Experiences

After you've brainstormed, there is a good chance you will still have to continue to mine your own life for inspiration. Unless your book is incredibly academic (like a textbook) or a biography of someone else, readers want to hear about you. Including stories from your own life does a couple of things. For one, it establishes a deeper connection to your reader. We find that this can be hardest for our industry expert professionals to implement, as they want their expertise and information to shine, keeping the focus off themselves. Your reader wants to know you, even if you are teaching them about something seemingly impersonal, like gardening. They want to know how you came to gardening, what's your connection to the material, what you find interesting about it, and potentially how it's changed your life in the same way it will change theirs. No matter what your professional or educational credentials are, people still want to learn from other people they know, like, and trust.

Secondly, including stories from your own life further establishes you as an expert. We have had so many clients say that they are wary of coming across as arrogant or "preachy" in their prescriptive book. Sometimes, if you get too carried away with instruction, it can feel like you're barking orders at the reader from your high horse. A great way to avoid this is to tell a story, preferably from your own life and experience, that illustrates your expertise. Here is where you can show instead of tell. Instead of *telling* the reader you know what you're talking about, *show* them. Author and communication expert Dorie Clark said, "demonstrate your expertise with stories, not words. Saying 'I'm great at pitching investors' sounds pretty egotistical. But sharing a compelling tale of how you rounded up seed funding allows others to deduce your skill without having to make it explicit."[2] James Clear opens *Atomic Habits* by telling the origin story of how he experimented and then discovered the ideas in the book, going all the way back to when he was in college. This establishes him in our minds as a trustworthy guide.

Memoirists, you will spend a lot of time here, as your book is mostly your own life story. And this process will likely be a little messier for you. Before you begin each chapter, reexamine your own life to find the stories you want to tell. Journaling might be a helpful practice to help jog your memory. But don't be surprised if you get deep into the writing process and remember something else that happened, one memory triggered by another. It is highly likely you will not have all of your stories and ideas decided before you start writing. That is okay and normal. Collect what you can ahead of time and get to work. And do not forget to not only dissect what happened to you, but explain what it meant to your journey, and thus for the reader's. Memoir is not a collection of stories of what happened to you, but what you did with what happened, what it meant for your life, and how it changed you.

Read for Inspiration

Let's talk about comp titles again. (See, you cannot escape them.) It's a good idea, as you are mining for content for your own book, to read them. Experts often reference the work of other writers in their field. It bolsters your argument and adds gravity to the writing to hear from someone other than the author. We've already extolled the virtue of reading and being familiar with other books in your genre, so we won't harp on it here except to say that your comp titles are not only good for understanding your market and mapping your own book, but also great for finding content ideas as well. For quotes, data, and stories that you can reference specifically (and cite appropriately) and for general inspiration.

But comps are not the only kind of books you can read to mine content for your own. *Any* genre of book can provide inspiration. Remember from chapter 5 that often great ideas are born from unlikely connections. There are illustrative stories and images in all kinds of books well outside your genre. Referencing them is a great way to add texture to the prose and make yourself look like a pro. Ryan Holiday is famous for this. Most of his books fall within the prescriptive genre of self-help and are riddled with stories, examples, and quotes from Roman emperors, dead presidents, CEOs of Fortune 500 companies, NFL players, and pop stars. Pick up a book to learn about how to overcome an obstacle, hear from Marcus Aurelius and Bill Belichick. Holiday can do this because he is a voracious reader. He sees connections all around him between what he's reading and what he's writing. He's constantly on the lookout for what or who he might come into contact with that is worthy of inclusion.

There is no limit to what kinds of books can inform your own. Read from your contemporaries, but don't be afraid to stray from them and also read whatever you are interested in. Inspiration for material can come from anywhere.

Peruse Magazines/Articles

Of course, books aren't the only other place you can go for content outside of your own mind. Online magazines and articles are some of the best places to find quotes and statistics, especially in a pinch. A quick Google search will turn up all kinds of returns about whatever you're looking for. Even just now, we searched "why do people want to write," which showed us a great quote and data-filled article from *Psychology Today*. If we find a passage we like, we could quote and credit the author of the article. For example, the author has kindly done some research already in preparation for his article and cited Joseph Epstein's study that taught us 81 percent of Americans feel they have a book in them.[3]

It might go without saying, but I'm going to say it anyway: Choose these magazines and online publications that you cite carefully. Use whichever you want if you are just reading for inspiration to shake some ideas loose. Heck, I (Liz) sometimes find myself deep down in Reddit threads learning all kinds of interesting things. But I wouldn't quote those people in my book. If you want to quote an article in your work, make sure it is reputable. Ideally, one with a recognizable name that has been around for a while. You can also use the blogs and personal websites of credible experts.

Interview Experts

As ghostwriters, we have thousands of hours of interviewing experience under our belts and know it to be one of the best ways to mine for content for your book. Lucinda Halpern interviewed dozens of writers, editors, and agents for her book *Get Signed*, resulting in many interesting quotes and points of view that supported her own. I had a similar honor when I worked on Grant Baldwin's book *The Successful Speaker*. I spoke to over twenty of the students who had successfully been through Grant's program and were now making money as professional speakers. Their experiences provided useful case studies and examples for the book, *and* subtly showed the reader the efficacy of Grant's ideas.

When you are running low on content ideas, or are just feeling like there's "too much of you" in a chapter, a great option to balance things out is to go interview someone else. You can also find interviews in magazines, videos, and books that others have conducted, which are helpful. But if at all possible, we encourage you to interview someone yourself. Not only is it great experience, it results in completely original material. It also forces you to think through what you'd like to know from an expert or case study and deepens your understanding of the topic. Try it! Reach out to people in your network or just cold email someone who might have a unique insight into your topic. You will probably find that many people, unless they are pretty famous and busy, will say yes. Everyone likes to be interviewed. And quick tip: if they're in the book, they are far more likely to endorse and promote it.

Anticipate Objections

One of the most overlooked ways to think about content, especially for prescriptive nonfiction writers, is to anticipate reader objections. Think about (and research!) what people "on the other side" of your argument would say. This is one of the best ways to understand the debates around your topic and different perspectives that readers might have.

You can also anticipate objections or potential roadblocks readers might come across during their transformation. Common ones for teaching books are phrases like "That sounds hard" or "That's too complicated" or "That's confusing." If you know a lot about a topic, it's easy to forget what a beginner might need to know. Think through how you can break things down, simplify them at every step. If you instruct your reader to build a website, what excuses might they come up with?

1. I don't know how.
2. I'm bad at tech.
3. What hosting service do I use?
4. Can I hire someone to help me?

. . . and many more. Address these in the writing. Answer their questions before they have the chance to get frustrated and talk themselves out of doing what they need to do.

We want to be clear that what we are not talking about here is "writing for the haters." Authors can go crazy imagining every negative thing anyone might say about their book. Don't do that. We're suggesting you anticipate the objections of *your* readers, the ones you want to help, and educate yourself on all sides of the debates in your space.

Search Databases, Studies, and Research Institutes

If you need research, statistics, case studies, or hard facts to back up a claim, there are no better places to look than online databases. These are most necessary in prescriptive books. You likely have beliefs and powerful statements you'd like to include in your chapters. Your opinion matters a lot. And, as you make your overarching argument throughout your book with smaller arguments in each chapter, that opinion is made much stronger with some cold hard facts. I could say, "In 2021, the Great Resignation led many US workers to quit for good." Or I could say, "In 2021, over 47 million people quit their jobs during The Great Resignation, more than 23 percent of the US workforce," and cite the US Bureau of Statistics in my endnotes.[4] Clearly, the latter is more powerful and effective in proving my point.

Like the magazines and websites that you cite in your work, you'll need to be careful here to only use reputable sources. Scopus, PubMed, Directory of Open Access Journals, and Public Library of Science are a few reliable places to look. Any statistics you find on a government website, from the Pew Research Center, or Gallup are going to be legitimate. You can also do your own research into the reliable institutions around your topic. The point is, data and statistics are fantastic to prove a point, but don't cite a number that keyboard warrior Joe Shmoe pulled out of the air. Reddit threads are for inspiration and ideas, not facts.

Tap into Artificial Intelligence

Imagine a big red flashing "proceed with caution" sign here. But this book would be incomplete without mentioning that AI can be a helpful tool in mining content for your book. You can jump on any number of open AI platforms and ask them everything from broad requests like "Tell me about yoga" to more specific prompts like "Give me five examples of yoga poses that help with anxiety and who invented each one." AI is a great tool for getting the ideas flowing and getting unstuck when you hit a wall. But it is not a place of reliable information. And of course, there are all kinds of plagiarism issues at play, so you never want to just copy and paste what you find in an AI database. Take what it turns up and go fact-check it yourself.

We like to use AI as a sounding board or conversation tool of sorts. You can ask it for data, stories, and examples when you're coming up empty. You can even ask its opinion on what you've written. Just take it all with a grain of salt and do your own fact checking. I'll be honest, I asked AI how to mine content for a book just to see what it came up with. It had some pretty decent ideas, though I'm pleased to say I'd already thought of most of them on my own. It was helpful to see I was on the right track.

The Art of Observation (Movies, Podcasts, Pop Culture, Politics, and the World at Large)

Content. Is. Everywhere. It's in the news, in your earbuds, and on your screens. It's in the cool breeze on your face and the rustle of the trees . . . okay I'm getting carried away. But only slightly. When you start looking for content, you will find it in everything. Just the other day, I was writing an article and quoted Meg Ryan playing Kathleen Kelly in *You've Got Mail*. She's slowly becoming friends with Joe Fox who put her sweet little bookstore out of business and says, "Anything else anything is, it ought to begin by being personal."[5] It's a good quote. And it happened to fit perfectly into my article about how the old idiom "It's not personal, it's business" is outdated and not true in this new age of business. I never would have discovered it if I wasn't watching a cozy movie on a fall night, believing I was wasting time. Because my eyes were open to the world around me and my article was top of mind, I made a surprising connection and enriched the work.

There will be a lot of starts and stops in this process. You will try stories that don't work, include statistics that you later discover don't say what you think they said, and maybe even argue yourself out of a once-held belief. That's okay. Adding in content to your work is like a puzzle. You have to try a few pieces sometimes before you find what fits exactly right. A final thought here: author Annie Dillard wrote, "One of the few things I know about writing is this: spend it all, shoot it, play it, lose it, all, right away, every time. Do not hoard what seems good for a later place in the book, or for another book; give it, give it all, give it now."[6] Include everything you can find that helps your reader. Do not save a single idea, especially on your first draft. Give them all the goods.

Keep trying and keep your eyes peeled. Stay open, stay curious. And then, put your head down and start writing. More on that next.

11

Set Writing Goals

There are only two kinds of authors: those who finish their book and those who don't. Catlin Tucker is a finisher.

I (Ariel) had the pleasure of working with Catlin on multiple best-selling books while I was an acquisitions editor. I was always impressed by her steady commitment to whatever deadline we set. She was realistic about what she could do, but once she set a target for herself, she never missed it. Never.

I often wished that I could get my other authors to be as reliable as Catlin was. At the time, she was working full-time as a teacher, traveling often to consult with schools, blogging regularly for multiple websites, completing her doctorate, raising two children, *and* writing a book. How could she possibly do everything so well? Once, I asked her what her secret was, hoping for some sexy tip I could include in my next author newsletter. Maybe she hides herself away on writing retreats and knocks out the whole draft in a week? Maybe she has an incredible book-mapping method that will change the course of writing history? Maybe she takes fancy supplements that give her superhuman clarity and turbo-typing skills?!

Here's what she told me:

"I write every day from 4–6 a.m. That's the only way it gets done."

Um. What? No thank you.

I confess I was surprised and a bit disappointed by her response—and yet, it made me admire her even more, too. For the first time, I realized the true grit and persistence and commitment that a seasoned professional writer brings to her craft. Catlin viewed her books as part of her job; they simply *had* to get done, and she created the time needed in her busy life to make it happen.

Steven Pressfield conveys a similar attitude in his writing classic *The War of Art*. He writes, "The writer is an infantryman. He knows that progress is measured in yards of dirt extracted from the enemy one day, one hour, one minute at a time and paid for in blood. The artist wears combat boots. He looks in the mirror and sees GI Joe."[1] The first time I read this line, I seriously considered buying myself a pair of combat boots to wear while writing—and then I remembered that comfy slippers are way more fun. But still, same idea.

This is the level of tenacity you need to finish your book. Once the book map is done, you are no longer in creative planning mode; you're now a soldier expected to carry out orders. You know what you need to write, and now it's time to execute.

All writers know that this level of persistence is required, and this is where many of us start to falter. We're inclined to look for gimmicks and secrets and quick fixes to help us shortcut our way to a finished draft. Some writing books and programs will try to help you make and keep your commitment to finishing your book by having you sign a written contract to yourself. Some will promise that you can write your entire book in a weekend or some other unrealistically short period of time. Some will create fancy calendars and tracking systems. For some people, these methods work well. For others, they're just a form of productive procrastination—one more distraction getting in the way of their writing.

That said, writing a book *is* a large project. If you want to get it done, we can give you some project management tools and advice to help you stay on track. In fact, we find it helpful to think of your book as a work project, rather than a fragile creative baby that you need to pamper and nurture. As professional ghostwriters, we've been forced to adopt this mentality. We literally can't afford to get precious about our books. If we spend months noodling over ideas and second-guessing ourselves, we don't get paid. While this takes some of the romance out of the process, the books also get done. Even if you're not being paid to complete your book on a timeline, this is now your job. In this chapter, we'll help you with the same strategies we use to get the job done.

Calculate Your Goals

You didn't expect this book to make you do some math, did you? We'll keep it easy—and yes, you can use your calculators.

First, you'll set a target word count for your book. Table 11.1 offers some typical word count ranges by genre. There's no "right" word count, but it's helpful to have something to aim for and a way to know when you're done. Having a word count goal can keep you moving forward when you feel stuck, and it can help you avoid getting too long-winded. Author Rob Fitzgerald writes, "A book should be as long as is necessary to convincingly deliver on its promise, but never any longer."[2]

Remember, most of the information in this book is *descriptive*, not prescriptive; we're not telling you your memoir *has* to be a certain length. We're just telling you that *most* memoirs fall in a certain range. Your book could end up being more or less than these numbers, but do pick a target number to aim for.

When in doubt, pick fifty thousand.

Write down your target word count.

Now let's figure out a target word count for your chapters.

Table 11.1.   **Typical Word Counts by Genre**

Genre	Typical Word Count Range
Prescriptive nonfiction	30,000–65,000 words
Memoir	60,000–80,000 words
Narrative nonfiction	80,000–100,000 words

Q&A

Q: Why not calculate an ideal page count?
A: Page count is fluid; it changes based on the paragraph spacing, size of the margins, trim size of the paper, font size, and so on. Word count is a fixed number that doesn't change based on any other variables.

We usually recommend allotting about 2,500 to 4,000 words (each) for your introduction and conclusion. Subtract that from your target word count. Then divide the number of words remaining by the number of chapters you have, and voila! You have an average number of words per chapter to aim for.

For example:

- If your target word count is 50,000 words
- Subtract 3,000 for the introduction = 47,000 words
- Subtract another 2,000 for the conclusion = 45,000
- Divide by the number of chapters you planned to have (let's say ten)
- Your average chapter should be about 4,500 words

Once you know about how long you want your book and each chapter to be, the other key piece of information you need is a target date for finishing.

Be Realistic!

There are so many programs out there that promise to teach you how to write a book in a weekend or thirty days or six weeks. There's even a book out there promising authors they can learn how to write a book in just twenty-four hours with the help of artificial intelligence. And maybe that sounds fun to you (it sounds terrifying to us!). But in all of our years of writing professionally and working with authors, we've never seen a high-quality book get done in this short amount of time. We imagine that most of you want to think deeply about every piece of your book, because you have something incredibly important to say, and you want to make sure it's the best it can be. Don't rush yourself. Ideas take time to evolve. Writing takes time to unfold.

Think about it this way: No publisher would ask for a book in that short amount of time; in fact, if you promise them a book in six weeks, they might give you some serious side-eye (unless it was already mostly written). Publishers are businesses, and they need accurate estimates of when they'll need to begin production on a book so that they can accurately forecast when they'll start to receive revenue from the book. They would rather estimate conservatively so that the book is more likely to come in on time. If it works for publishers, who have a lot of money invested in books and need to make sure they recoup that investment, it can work for you!

The other reason to be realistic in setting a target finish date is for the sake of your own confidence. We don't just want you to write a great book; we want you to *enjoy* the process and watch your confidence grow as you make progress toward your goal. Setting an unrealistic finish date can make many authors feel inadequate if they can't achieve that impossible date. Instead, you'll be more confident, and therefore more likely to actually meet your date, if it feels doable and realistic. Author Annie Dillard was a fan of the slower pace of writing and wrote in her book *The Writing Life*, "Most writers might well stop berating themselves for writing at a normal, slow pace."[3] Good writing takes time.

With that said, pick an ideal target finish date—we recommend that it be no less than three months in the future, and no more than a year. If you put your finish date *too* far into the future, you might not ever feel the urgency you need to get it done.

When in doubt, pick six months.

Write down your target finish date.

Divide It Up

At this point, you have a few options for ways you can divvy up your work into smaller segments, depending on how you like to work. Do you want to try to write every day? Or batch your work based on when you know you might have some time? Here are a couple methods to consider.

Set a Weekly/Daily Word Count Goal

Let's say you've given yourself six months to complete a fifty-thousand-word book. That would be:

- 8,333 words per month
- 2,083 words per week
- 416 words per day (if you're writing five days/week)

Set a Chapter Goal

You may instead want to write each of your chapters in one week, and spread those weeks out over six months. Again, for the sake of this example, assume you're writing ten chapters in six months. Six months has twenty-six weeks, so you can easily spread out the writing of your chapters in that time—just make sure you're accomplishing almost two chapters (1.6, to be precise) per month in order to get the book done by your target date.

Test, Then Decide

Another method that works well is to give yourself a test period. Write the first chapter and see how long it takes you. If the first chapter takes a month, then you know you actually need ten months to write all ten chapters—or you need to pick up the pace in order to get the book done in six months. In chapter 12, we'll talk about writing routines to help you stay motivated and come to the page everyday ready to write.

Do What Works for You—But Do Something

Remember, despite all our planning and the beautiful book map you created, this is the point where most authors fall behind. That's because realizing your vision is actually very hard work. Our goal in this book is to prepare you for success, but we can't actually do the work for you. (Well, we can, if you want us to ghost it for you!) If you want to write the book yourself, then you'll have to learn to love the work itself.

Our best advice is to find a rhythm that feels fun, life-giving, and doable for you. Note that the writing itself won't always feel fun or life-giving—much like going to the gym, the writing is often painstaking and heavy and annoying. But you'll never regret showing up. And much like exercising, the more you do it, the easier it becomes. Just as you have to find an exercise routine that works for you—maybe rock climbing or weight lifting or salsa dancing or yoga—you also have to find a writing routine that works for you. That's the topic of chapter 12.

Hold Yourself Accountable

Many authors ask us to help them stay accountable to their goals. They say things like, "I want you to hold my feet to the fire" or "I'm really deadline driven." We get it. Like we said, as ghostwriters, if we don't meet our deadlines, we don't get paid. But the truth is that the only person who can get the work done on your book (assuming you don't want to hire a ghostwriter!) is you.

Here are a few common accountability methods. They can work marginally well—but only if you want them to. You'll have to decide for yourself which ones might work for you, and which ones won't. Use your past experiences and experiment to help you decide whether you need one of these tools. Maybe you don't!

- **Set rewards for yourself.** Personally, this is a favorite strategy for us. I (Ariel) treat myself to my favorite guilty pleasure fast food (Chipotle) every time I finish a chapter. I also love new clothes, so I'll indulge in a trip to Madewell or a local boutique when I meet larger milestones. These rewards work well for me because these are luxuries I don't (often) otherwise indulge in. Your rewards don't have to be physical goods, either. Reward yourself with a nice long bath or a long walk along the closest body of water. Pick your favorite flowers to decorate your bookshelf.
- **Work with a book coach.** Good coaches can help you set goals, problem solve, think through and plan your writing time, remove distractions, and provide positive feedback and reinforcement for your efforts. Just remember that a coach can't do the work for you!
- **Join a writing group.** Writing groups are often less expensive than working one-on-one with a coach, but come with the same benefit of feedback, problem

solving, and encouragement. The downside of writing groups is that you're expected to read and give feedback to others as well—which you might enjoy, but does take some time away from your own work. Writing groups also often lack the expertise of a coach. We recommend joining one if what you primarily want is encouragement; writing groups are great for that!

- **Go on a writing retreat.** Sometimes, authors do need to step away from their normal environment so they can focus on their work. Writing retreats are perfect for meeting that need! It doesn't have to be expensive or lengthy; sometimes just a weekend in an Airbnb can help you make incredible progress.

Again, not all these methods will work for you. Try a few, but keep in mind that no one can make you do the work you don't want to do. That said—assuming you're still here and this chapter hasn't scared you away—in chapter 12, we'll help you adopt writing routines and rituals that make the work feel fun and life-giving.

12

Establish Writing Rhythms

Now that you know how many words you need to write to meet your goals, let's talk about how to get them on the page. We begin with an annoying yet truest of true truths: there is no right way to write.

Van Gogh worked in spurts of sleepless nights almost driving himself mad. Greats like Fitzgerald and Hemingway famously showed up to the page at the same time every morning.[1] When Cheryl Strayed's best-selling memoir *Wild* was still mostly unfinished three weeks before her deadline, she locked herself in a remote cabin away from her kids and husband to "write like a motherfucker."[2] Best-selling author, thought leader, and prolific blogger Seth Godin never answers questions about his writing routine because he doesn't want anyone to take it as the "right" way when it's only what works for him. And so we'll say again: there is no right way, only what works for you.

That being said, there are writing rhythms that are largely helpful to many authors, including us. There are habits you can form and techniques to implement to help you go from the blank page to a full manuscript, and hopefully even enjoy the process along the way.

Get Prepped

Author and psychologist Dr. Benjamin Hardy said that the most productive days start the night before.[3] In the case of writing a book, the best writing days usually begin with decent sleep the night before. We all have life constraints that sometimes prevent us from implementing our ideal routines. Perhaps you have factors like young children or anxiety that interrupt your sleep. But to the best of your ability, get some good rest before your creative work. Your brain needs it to make those amazing contextual and temporal connections between ideas. There are entire books on morning and evening routines (like *Daily Rituals*, *The Miracle Morning*, and *Deep Work*). We recommend those if you want to learn what some successful people do in the morning and evenings to operate at their highest level.

Before you drift off to sleep, it can also be helpful to write down your intentions for your writing session the next day. What chapter do you plan to write? What is your word count goal? What stories and ideas do you want to cover? Are there any unanswered questions you need to research? This gives your brain something to "do" while you sleep. We're serious. Your subconscious mind wanders while you sleep. It sorts, consolidates, and stores new information. If you give it a problem to solve right before you drift off, it can even help you find a solution. Why not set your mind to focusing on your writing before you're even up and sentient enough to type?

After you get up and do whatever your morning routine requires, it can be helpful to incorporate some form of journaling to clear the metaphorical mental cobwebs. Julia Cameron's morning pages practice, popularized by her book *The Artist's Way*, has been beloved and touted by many kinds of creatives for decades. It involves free-writing three handwritten pages about anything and everything on your mind before digging into work. People report many epiphanies after incorporating this routine.[4] They become poets, start composing music, make better arguments in court, and even decide they want out of relationships. But know that any kind of journaling or cobweb clearing is helpful. The exact method isn't as important as the habit of clearing your mind of distractions and worries before sitting down to work. And many find it constructive to literally clear them by taking them out of your mind and onto the page. This makes room for the work of writing your book that you've set out to do.

Create a Space and Time

We've said that there is no right way to write, except that, to have a book, you must actually do some writing. Like we talked about in chapter 11, we recommend treating it like a work project or a job. If you don't show up to your job, you will get fired. If you do not show up for your book, regularly, it will never get done. So create a space and time for that to happen. Virginia Woolf extolled the virtue of having "a room of one's own" in which to write. But if that isn't possible for you in your current life circumstances, don't fret. Any kind of space set aside especially for your writing will do. It may be just a particular chair you like, or a spot on the couch. It doesn't even have to be in your house. Maybe there's a nook at a coffee shop that feels especially inspiring. When I (Liz) was in college, I had a particular chair at the library that I insisted on sitting in when I studied and became borderline superstitious about it. Whatever it is, set aside a space that is meaningful to you, especially for working on your book.

Set a time. There is no magic to this one. Put it on the calendar and make it happen, like an appointment you cannot miss. As we discussed in chapter 11, this may take some experimentation. We don't care if you need to write every day, or if there is only one day a week when you can get it done. The point is to make it happen regardless. According to research, your brain is most primed for creativity right after sleep.[5] That's why so many authors' routines involve writing in the morning. But then again, plenty don't. Tim Ferriss has said many times that he loves writing late into the night and early morning. Find what works for you and put it on the calendar.

Make a promise to yourself and keep it. Sit your butt down and get it done. Sometimes, it's just as simple as that. Brené Brown said, "The middle is messy, but it's also where the magic happens."[6] You're deep in the magic now. You cannot wait for the muse to show up and must create that magic for yourself by showing up and moving forward. The conditions will almost never be exactly right and you cannot let that stop you from showing up when you said you would. You do the work to write no matter what. That's how books get written.

Have a Ritual

I (Liz) find it helpful to have a short ritual I employ every time I'm putting myself in writing mode. For me, this looks like simply lighting a candle and meditating on the ideal reader for the book I'm working on. I think about the transformation of the book, and the smaller transformation of the chapter I'm working on. I imagine the ideal reader and how I want them to feel after reading it. This helps me get into creative mode and set aside my other worries of the day. It also directs my focus on the most important thing: serving my readers.

Your ritual can be anything you want it to be. Many writers put on certain music, go for a walk, eat a particular meal, recite affirmations, exercise, or drink water before they sit down to do the work. I even read about one author who insists pooping before writing helps him think better. It doesn't matter what it is, a ritual can signal your brain that it's time to write. The book *Daily Rituals* is chock full of ideas if you want more inspiration from some of the greats.

Do Not Fear the Shitty First Draft

One of the hardest things for new writers to understand is that the first draft is going to be bad. It's going to be bad, bad. It might even be bad, bad, BAD. And ... that's good! Well, maybe not *good*, but it's normal and where we all start. Absolutely nothing is as intimidating as a blank page, so do whatever you have to do to get some words on there. You cannot work with nothing. Plus, with your book map in hand, things cannot turn out *that* poorly. We promise. Since you have a plan, you are already ahead of the curve. And even your messy word vomit is guaranteed to be workable. Even if it does feel like you are just vomiting words onto the page, because of your map and grasp of your book's transformation, the words will more or less be in the right place and all aiming in the same direction. Your shitty first draft won't be *that* shitty. Less shitty than most. That's the beauty of book mapping. And don't worry, you are going to edit the thing many times over (more on that in chapter 13). That is not your concern right now. Your only goal on draft one is to get the words on the page to the best of your ability, following your book map.

Do not fear the shitty first draft. Embrace it. It is the only place to begin. You cannot get good unless you give yourself permission to be bad. So open a Word document and start writing words, even if they're bad words.

Get Unstuck

Inevitably, no matter how prepped and ready you are, you will get stuck in the writing process. You've probably heard this referred to as "writer's block." This simply means that you have sat down to write, you might even know what you want to say and . . . the words won't come. They are log-jammed inside your mind and your fingers are paralyzed. It happens to the best of us. Here are a few things you can do.

1. **Record yourself speaking**. One of the best ways to get the creative juices flowing again is to switch mediums. You can still make progress on your book even if you are not typing words into your word document. With your book map in front of you, try recording yourself talking through your ideas and stories. You can even have these conversations transcribed and edit them like your manuscript. "Talking out your book" does not usually result in a great enough first draft without a tremendous amount of editing, but it does serve as an effective way to get unstuck when your fingers seem to betray you.

2. **Move your body.** Any form of physical movement is great for creativity. Maybe you've heard the phrase "get in your body" when your mind is giving you trouble. That's because exercise has been shown to heighten your imagination and help you come up with new ideas. Our brains change in response to physical activity, in part because of the extra blood flow and oxygen.[7] There are also countless studies about how great some sunshine and fresh air are for our mental health.[8] When you are stuck in your work, get up and move around. Bonus points if you do it outside.

3. **Change up your surroundings.** Though we encourage you to have a designated space to write, we can all stagnate occasionally. If the words aren't flowing, another idea is to literally go somewhere else. Humans are highly affected by our environment, and if you've been sitting in writer's block shame at your desk for the last couple of days, it might be time to shake it up. Try working in a different spot, maybe within your own home or somewhere else.

4. **Free write.** Similar to journaling, sometimes free-writing can be the release you need to get things moving

again. If you are able to free yourself from the pressure of writing your book and just write in no particular order with no agenda, it can unlock that creative door that seems to be jammed. You can even write about the same topic or same chapter, just tell yourself you're brain-dumping about it, not officially "working on your book." It might sound silly, but our brains can be kinda dumb. This is a way to trick yours into working again by taking some pressure off. Much of the goal of this comes back to withholding judgment. The pressure to "get it right" or constantly meditating on how big and important your project is, is debilitating. Try writing only for the sake of writing and see what comes out. You might just be surprised at how usable some of it is.

5. **Do something fun.** As professional writers, we have been up against deadlines countless times, feeling like we need to use every last second to work until the end and make sure it's perfect. This is a recipe for burnout. One of the best things you can do for yourself when you feel like the words just aren't turning out how you want them to is to go do something fun. Even and especially when you feel like you "can't" or "don't deserve it." You *do* deserve it. The work will get done whether you make yourself miserable or not. Go get a dopamine hit and let yourself enjoy it. As we mentioned in chapter 11, indulge in one of your accountability rewards. We promise that it will actually improve your writing.

Here are some additional fun, quick tips to aid you in the writing process. These aren't mandatory, but if you're looking to give yourself the best shot at finishing your manuscript, consider incorporating some of these into your routine.

Tips and Tricks

1. **Clear the clutter.** Research suggests visual distractions can be a significant source of stress. Before you begin, or if you're stuck, try clearing out your workspace. You could organize other areas as well. One of my favorite things to do when I'm blocked creatively is go organize my closet. It's rewarding and gives me a quick win, which makes me feel like I can keep going.

2. **Eat something.** Writing with a grumbling stomach is no fun. Take care of yourself and eat something. A word of caution, though: Getting up to get snacks is also a popular procrastination technique. The late, great Rachel Held Evans used to write with a notecard on her desk that said, "The next sentence is NOT in the refrigerator."[9]

3. **Set a timer.** We love the pomodoro technique, which involves working in twenty-five-minute stretches of work broken up by five-minute breaks. Longer breaks are taken after four consecutive work intervals. The exact method you use doesn't matter as much as the fact that you force yourself to sit and write until that dang timer goes off. Research shows we've only got about three great hours of solid work in us a day, anyway.[10] Ensure you're making progress toward your word count goals by sitting down for a certain amount of time.

4. **Paint your nails.** Okay, you might find this silly, but I'm telling you, there's something to it. It's like how fitness people tell you buying cute workout clothes will incentivize you to exercise. Since you're always half-looking at your fingers in your periphery as you write, they might as well be cute. Maybe it'll even encourage you to use them for more book writing. It's worth a shot.

5. **Put on some good music.** This largely comes down to preference, but not many writers we know like to write in silence. Similar to exercise, research also suggests that music can help with creativity by activating different areas of your brain. It helps you get into that "flow state" writers are always striving for. Popular choices are instrumental and acoustic playlists, or sometimes even background noises like waves or thunderstorms. Anything that feels soothing but not distracting. Experiment with different sounds to get yourself in the writing mood.

Writing to the end of a manuscript takes real work. You won't hear us ever say otherwise. But it can also be fun and incredibly rewarding. Take the ideas in this chapter and try out a few to help you on your way to fulfilling your dream of finishing your book. Then, with all those wonderful words that you've dreamt of writing for so long finally on the page, it's time to make them really shine.

13

Edit Your Masterpiece

At some point—be it six months, one year, or three years down the road—you will have finished your manuscript. Before you go any further, we hope that you take time to celebrate this important milestone and reflect on how you feel. This reflection is key to becoming a better writer and preparing you for your next book.

I'm sorry, what?? You're probably thinking. Yes, the next book. Because, remember: Hungry Authors have a long-term perspective. They know that each book is just preparation for the next one. You will write many books in your life! You've only written the first one.

So how do you feel? Ask yourself these questions:

- What was the hardest part about writing this book?
- What was the best part of writing this book?
- What are you proud of?
- What do you feel you could have done differently?
- How do you want to celebrate your accomplishment?

Take a Break to Shift Your Perspective

No matter how you feel after finishing your first draft, we recommend that you take a break from it for a while. Why, you ask?

Taking a break is about changing your perspective. By putting your manuscript away for a while, you'll be able to come back to it with fresh eyes. You'll be able to distance yourself from the writing of it and experience the draft as your reader might. You'll notice things you never saw before when you were in it every day. This change in perspective is absolutely critical in order to accomplish the goal of this chapter: editing your own manuscript.

Only you can say how long a break you need—two weeks, a month, a year? On his podcast, *The Daily Stoic*, author Ryan Holiday shared that Joan Didion had a habit of putting her manuscripts away for a year before going back to edit and publish them. Her discipline (because it does require discipline to not touch your work for so long!) inspired him to take a similar year-long break after he finished writing the third manuscript in his Stoic virtues series.[1] We don't necessarily recommend a year; we recommend taking however long you need to accomplish that perspective shift, without losing your passion and excitement for the work or missing your deadline!

However long you choose, once you've gotten used to sleeping in again and stopped having nightmares about what readers will think about your chapters, it's time to head back to work, this time to edit.

Why Edit Your Own Work?

You might be wondering why we recommend editing your own work—after all, isn't that what professional editors are for? Ryan Holiday himself writes in *Perennial Seller*: "Nobody creates flawless drafts. And nobody creates better second drafts without the intervention of somebody else. Nobody."[2]

That's all well and true; we're not here to say you don't need an editor or that you shouldn't hire one. You'll never be able to achieve the outside perspective and clarity that someone else will about your book. You absolutely will need an editor.

But we are here to say that editing your own work *first* will make the book and your experience working with an editor so much better. Plus, you'll learn to spot your own mistakes earlier, ultimately improving your book and your writing skills as you go.

Here are the benefits of learning to edit your own work:

- While you can't cut out editors from the process entirely (and you don't want to!), you might be able to limit the number of revisions needed—and therefore the money you need to spend on editors.
- The better you can make the draft you send to an editor, the higher quality an edit they can provide. Editors can't take a shitty first draft and make it great, but they can take a pretty good second draft and make it great.
- You'll become a more attractive partner to editors and publishers when you consistently prove that you can turn in fairly clean drafts.
- As mentioned, you'll improve your own skills as a writer!

Tips and Tricks

- Seriously, take a break from your manuscript. Don't skip this!!
- Schedule time to edit in small batches.
- Keep a thesaurus handy.
- Print out your manuscript and grab your favorite color pens and highlighters.
- Find a software program that can read your manuscript out loud to you. Our ears can often pick up on things our eyes miss!
- Take breaks whenever you need to throughout all three phases. This is hard work!

Three Phases of Editing

In this chapter, we'll teach you how to edit your manuscript in three phases inspired by our friend Jeff Goins, who tells authors to "make it work, make it true, and make it pretty":

- Phase 1: Make It Work
- Phase 2: Make It Right
- Phase 3: Make It Pretty

Phase 1: Make It Work

When you return to your manuscript, you'll want to take the thirty-thousand-foot view. Your goal in this phase is to reconnect and realign with the transformation you planned back in chapter 6. Does that transformation still hold true? Is it what you actually wrote?

Often, authors are dismayed to find that their Transformation Tale has changed a bit. That's normal. As much as we like to plan in advance, writing is always an act of discovery. It's likely that some things will have shifted. We recommend skimming through the manuscript again as you keep your original Transformation Tale handy next to you (it can be helpful to print it out!). Compare it to your book map. Notice what has changed and what is still the same. If your Transformation Tale felt a bit fuzzy to you at the beginning of this process, it's likely that it's come into sharper focus now. Update your Transformation Tale to reflect this more holistic and cohesive understanding of your book.

It's also likely that you'll notice some areas where your book has drifted off course. Perhaps in chapter 4, you included a diatribe on something you're really passionate about, but upon reviewing your book through the lens of your transformation, you realize that that diatribe doesn't actually contribute. It'll need to be cut.

We don't say this lightly; cutting your material is one of the hardest parts of the editing process. It hurts. There is suffering. There is grief—even more so because you must choose it yourself.

The phrase "kill your darlings" has become synonymous with the editing phase and has been repeated *ad nauseum* by editors and writers for years. The earliest version of this phrase was actually penned by Sir Arthur Quiller-Crouch in his treatise "On the Art of Writing" in 1914: "Whenever you feel an impulse to perpetrate a piece of exceptionally fine writing, obey it—whole-heartedly—and delete it before sending your manuscript to press. *Murder your darlings.*"[3] This is a little harsh and we generally don't recommend murdering things, no matter how extraneous they may be to your purpose—especially good words that could be found a new home for later on. Generally, we believe books and authors are in the business of saving lives, and that goes for our words, too. Unless you're feeling particularly angry and vengeful, then rest assured that you don't have to actually murder your darlings. You can save them instead.

Keep a separate document handy and title it "Darlings." This is your Darlings Document. In it, your darlings aren't actually killed but rather stored for safekeeping so that you can repurpose them for something else later. We find that this is a gentler, easier way for many authors (including us!) to find the courage to cut what needs to be cut.

Still other sections you might realize need to be shifted or moved to another chapter in order to better align with the overall transformation of the book. Implement all of these big picture edits now. It's better to make big edits, like moving chapters or cutting your darlings, before editing at the paragraph or sentence level so that you don't waste time editing something that might need to be cut!

In this phase of editing, you'll also want to assess each individual chapter. Does each chapter successfully accomplish its own little transformation? Are there any pieces of the argument that you might have missed? Is each chapter's hook engaging and interesting? Do you have a good balance of stories and exposition, for prescriptive nonfiction books? For creative nonfiction, does each chapter build on the next?

Resist the urge in this phase of editing to get into the nitty gritty details. You may notice some spelling errors, awkward phrasing, or obvious little details that you missed. If you're reading the manuscript on paper, simply highlight or circle them in your favorite colorful pen and move on. You'll come back to them in the next phase.

Once you've gone through the book again at this high level and made your big-picture edits, then we recommend writing a one-sentence, one-paragraph, and one-page summary of your book. These summaries will come in handy for your next steps with the book, like writing a proposal or self-publishing (which we'll cover in part IV). But more importantly, this exercise will help you start articulating your book in a reader-focused way. Going forward, you're going to be often asked, "What's your book about?" and we want you to be able to answer that question with confidence, including only the most interesting, important information for your potential readers.

Here are some helpful templates to help you craft these summaries. Remember, these templates should be a starting

One-Sentence Summary Template

"This [WHAT] does [WHAT] for [WHO], so that/because [WHY]."

One-Paragraph Summary Template

- Sentence 1: One-sentence hook (steal this from your intro!)
- Sentence 2: Who is your hero and what is their current state?
- Sentence 3: How does this problem get solved?
- Sentence 4: What is the transformation by the end of the book?
- Sentence 5: End with the one-sentence summary you just wrote above.

One-Page Summary Template

- Paragraph 1: Short hook (two to three sentences)
- Paragraph 2: The current state (Who is your hero, what do they want, and what is stopping them from getting it?) (one paragraph)
- Paragraph 3: The in-between (one paragraph)
- Paragraph 4: The transformation (one paragraph)
- End with the one-sentence summary you just wrote above.

point; you don't have to follow them word for word or point for point! Adapt them to fit your book—but make sure that all of the necessary pieces of information are there.

When you've finished making your big picture edits and writing your summaries, then it's time to move on to phase 2: Make It Right.

Phase 2: Make It Right

The goal in phase 2 is to refine *how* you're communicating your message. Here, you'll want to reread the entire manuscript thoroughly. Again, printing it out can help, as well as using software to have your computer read it out loud to you. As you read, your top three concerns are:

- Engagement: Is it interesting?
- Content: Is it true and correct?
- Voice: Does it sound like me? How will readers respond to it?

Let's tackle these concerns one by one.

Engagement

Author Heather Wolpert-Gawron is an educator. She writes about student engagement:

> When I think of engagement, I don't think of "fun." I think of all elements as "engaging," as in all elements coming together and ready to go. I think of Captain Picard and his "Engage!" before the Enterprise speeds off to an adventure. I think of trains coupling before being pulled and picking up steam. Engagement isn't always about what makes a kid smile; it's about engaging the machine that is the brain.[4]

Replace "kid" with "reader," and the same truths apply here to writing books—especially nonfiction books.

Engagement is about inviting the reader into a state of flow—the sweet spot between making the reader work too hard to understand something and telling them so much that all sense of mystery and wonder has been sucked out of the pages. Remember, readers love reading for the sense of being transported, totally engrossed in whatever the author has to say. As writers, we create this sense by making the reader's brain work in just the right way. We do this by making the reader *curious*, making them wonder about what's coming next, and giving them dopamine-rewarding *aha* moments. These little bits of brain work don't actually feel like work; they feel interesting and exciting.

And trust us, engagement is not just for fiction! Nonfiction books, both prescriptive and creative, can be just as enjoyable as fiction, if written well.

This is (again) where returning to your comp books can be helpful. Think about what you enjoy most about them. How do the authors keep your interest the whole way through? What makes you stick with a book instead of giving up on it (besides sheer willpower, we hope!)? How might you apply the same strategies to your own book?

In prescriptive nonfiction, keep a lookout for places where you should balance exposition and data with stories and examples. Pay attention to your transitions—the magical glue between chapters and ideas that should keep readers turning the page. Are you reminding readers how one chapter leads to another, and how together, they contribute to the overall transformation of the book?

In creative nonfiction, are you beginning each section and each chapter with forward momentum, a sense of urgency that will propel the reader to continue? Does the story zoom in on the most important moments and zoom out on the background information and context? How are you ending each chapter on a tantalizing hook for the next one?

Content

Our next concern in phase 2 is ensuring that the content is sound—specifically for prescriptive nonfiction books. When you make a claim like, "Starbucks is America's favorite coffee shop," are you backing it up with evidence? Can you show data about Starbucks' revenue versus other coffee shops, for example? Make sure that you are anticipating objections and addressing them up front. For example, imagine the reader's possible arguments with that claim and the data you presented: *Well, sure, Starbucks may be the highest-grossing coffee chain, but could that be because of accessibility rather than preference? If other coffee shops were equally accessible and convenient, would people prefer those instead?* Valid points! How would you respond to them? Tackle those possible counterpoints up front. If you don't, your readers will bring them up in the form of one- and two-star reviews on Amazon.

When rereading your content, you should also check to make sure that you're being explicit about how ideas are connected. In our experience, this can be one of the most challenging issues for authors to spot in their own work. That's because, as authors, we know exactly what we want to say, and our brain tends to automatically fill in the gaps for us—so we don't see the ways that we might lose the reader.

Here's an over-obvious example of how ideas often need more connective tissue between them:

> Finding things to do with your kids during the summer when they're out of school is tough. But if you save up money throughout the school year and plan ahead, you can take them to Disneyland.

Sure, you probably understand that the author is positioning Disneyland as the solution to the problem of how to keep kids entertained over the summer—but as readers, we see immediately that it would be stronger if the author expanded a bit to connect these two ideas more strongly:

Finding things to do with your kids during the summer when they're out of school is tough. Taking them to a theme park like Disneyland is one option that the whole family can enjoy, although it can be prohibitively expensive for some families. If it's within your means, one way to get around the cost might be to save up money throughout the school year.

Spotting these gaps in logic might be difficult for you at first—but over time, if you start paying attention to how you're connecting ideas in your writing, you'll get better at noticing when you need to be more explicit.

Voice

The third question to ask yourself as you're rereading (or re-rereading) your manuscript is *does it sound like me?* Does it have the tone that you want to use with your reader? How will it make your reader feel?

These questions are answered with voice.

Your voice as an author is one of the seemingly most ephemeral aspects of your manuscript, and yet it's often the X factor that will make readers fall in love with your writing. Veteran literary agent Rachelle Gardner says, "Your writer's voice is the expression of YOU on the page."[5] Voice is the end result of the choices you make about what words to use in what order. Voice includes elements like:

- The tone, or attitude, you convey toward your reader. (Does it feel condescending, or friendly?)
- Emotion
- Rhythm
- Humor
- Point of view (are you writing in the intimate first person, or a more distant, formal third person?)

Unlike facts that you can fact check, voice is subjective. It's often described with words like, "brusque," "straightforward,"

"lyrical," "contemplative," "punchy," "irreverent," "warm"—
words that describe what it *feels like* for the reader to read your
book. It's helpful to ask yourself: How do I want my reader to
feel when reading my book? You might want them to laugh,
to cry, to feel a pang of bittersweetness, to feel encouraged or
informed.

As the famous quote goes, people will forget what you
said. They'll forget what you wrote. But what stays with readers long after they've finished reading your book is how it
made them *feel*.

So, in this phase of editing, ask yourself: How am I making my reader feel?

Phase 3: Make It Pretty

When you've made it through phase 2 and the manuscript
is as correct, engaging, and *you* as you can make it, then it's
time to do a final run-through to check for more basic issues
like spelling and grammar. Even though this may seem like
the "easy stuff," you want to save it for last because in phases
1 and 2, you may be doing a significant amount of rewriting.
There's no point in spell-checking a section of your manuscript that needs to be rewritten anyway!

And we have good news here, too: Don't try to do this
yourself. By this point, you've spent so much time with the
manuscript you probably can't spot all of the basic errors—
and you don't have to. There are too many great online tools
that can do this better than you can anyway. Simply find one
you like, copy and paste sections of your manuscript into the
tool, and let it fix those simple mistakes for you!

With that said, you (or your AI tool) are not going to catch
every mistake. The book will *not* be perfect by this point. Here
us loud and clear: You *still* need to work with an editor who
can see things that you, for all your passes, will not see. But
by going through these phases first, your editor will be able to
help you take your manuscript from *meh* to *wow!*

164 / Chapter 13

Q&A

Q: Should You Use Beta Readers?
A: Yes, if you have time! If you're on deadline for a publisher (more on that in part IV), then you may not have time for beta readers to read your manuscript and send you detailed feedback about it, and then for you to implement their feedback. But if you do have the time, then it's absolutely worthwhile to double check your own impulses and instincts by soliciting comments from your ideal readers. Briefly, let's answer some of the most common logistical questions about working with beta readers.

Q: When should you send your manuscript to beta readers?
A: After you finish a self-edit of the draft, following the three phases in this chapter! That way your beta readers are less likely to get distracted by things that you could spot and fix on your own (or with the help of AI). You want beta readers to use their energy helping you find things that would otherwise be missing.

Q: How many beta readers should you use?
A: Too much feedback can be overwhelming; too little can leave you without any consensus to follow. We recommend aiming for five to seven beta readers whom you feel confident will give the manuscript their full attention and honest input.

Q: How long should you give beta readers to read your manuscript?
A: Three to four weeks is optimal; enough time that they don't have to rush, but not so much time that they forget or procrastinate too much!

Q: What kind of feedback should you ask for?
A: We recommend sending your readers a list of specific questions you have about the manuscript—likely open-ended, phase 2-level questions. Warning: If you give readers yes-or-no questions, it's likely they'll give you yes-or-no answers! Think carefully about how you word your questions to make sure you get helpful answers. You'll want to ask them things like:

- Which parts of the manuscript were most engaging, and why?
- Which parts of the manuscript were most boring or hard to read, and why? What do you think I could do to improve them?
- Which chapters' hook(s) did you enjoy the most, and why?
- What are your top takeaways from the book?
- What do you think is the biggest change from the beginning of the book to the end?
- What questions do you still have about [your story/topic] that I should be sure to address for readers?
- How did you feel reading the book? How would you describe the tone and voice throughout the manuscript?

Q: Should you compensate beta readers?
A: This is up to you and your budget. Spending time to give you quality feedback is a significant "ask" for people who have busy lives and work of their own to do! Use your discretion, but at the very least, we recommend offering to buy them a coffee.

Q: How do you sort through everyone's feedback?
A: Don't feel like you have to take everyone's feedback! Instead, try to look for consensus among your readers. If one person has a strong opinion, that might simply be their

opinion. But if multiple readers make the same recommendation, you should probably take it into consideration! If it's something you disagree with, then it may be that you need to address that possible concern up front for the reader within the manuscript.

Now, after making your own edits and working with an editor, it's time to look forward to putting your book out into the world for others to read!

Part IV

PITCH OR PUBLISH

The only right way to publish your book is the one that gets it done.

That is to say, there are lots of right ways to publish your book. A lot of authors get hung up on making this decision, agonizing over which publishing road to take. It's one of the most common questions we get asked: *Should I self-publish, or shoot for traditional publishing?*

To be fair, it's an important question; it'll determine how you spend your time, energy, and potentially money in the next several months. But here's what it won't do: It won't determine how successful your book is or isn't. And it certainly won't have a bearing on your talent as a writer, the worthiness of your message, or your value as a human being.

Too many authors believe that how they publish their book says something about who they are. And it's just not true. We get it; rejection stings. But to allow it to have any bearing on your identity and value? To allow someone else's totally subjective opinion to dictate how you do your job? No. That's where we have to draw the line.

If you've made it this far in the book—meaning you have a truly *great* idea, you've designed a meaningful transformation for the hero of your story, and you've written the dang book—then you owe it to yourself and to your readers to see it through. The Hungry Author's mindset is not "traditional publishing or bust." It's "How do I make this happen?"

Remember, you are a working stiff. As our friend, author Kent Sanders, likes to say, "Writing is an incredibly blue collar thing to do." You're here to do a job. And the next task in your job is to determine your next steps for bringing your book into the world.

Traditional vs. Self-Publishing vs. Hybrid

You're standing at a crossroads. In front of you are three possible paths: self-publishing, traditional publishing, and hybrid publishing. The first path looks like a bushwhacker, with overgrown thickets and tree roots and rocks in the way. The second path looks smooth and easy, but has a big scary gate and an army of gatekeepers standing in front of it. The third path has billboards plastered all over it offering a smooth journey for a nominal fee—and frankly, you're a little suspicious. Soon you'll learn that looks aren't everything, and none of these paths are quite what they seem. They *all* lead to the same destination, though: a published book.

Each of these publishing models attempts to answer two questions:

- Who bears the most financial risk for this investment (and therefore receives most of the reward)?
- Who does which parts of the work?

Each model has its pros and cons. By saying yes to one publishing model, you can look forward to enjoying the "pros," but you'll also need to accept the "cons" of that model.

In part IV, we'll introduce you to each model and help you understand how they work so that you can choose your next right steps. You have the immense power and responsibility of owning your destiny.

14

Do-It-Yourself

Self-Publishing

There is nothing more hungry than a good ol' fashioned DIY project. If you've been thinking that self-publishing is the red-headed stepchild of the publishing world, hang tight. We think this will change your mind.

The practice of writing, manufacturing (or paying to manufacture), and then disseminating a work of your own creation has a long and rich history—longer, even, than most traditional publishing companies! Benjamin Franklin, one of the United States' founding fathers, was a prolific publisher of his own works, assembling and printing a new edition of his famous *Poor Richard's Almanac* every year for twenty-five years, from 1733–1758.[1] In the 1790s, the poet William Blake also wrote, illustrated, and then printed his own books of poetry, including *Songs of Innocence*, using a technique of his own design that he called "illuminated printing."[2] Even Jane Austen paid a printer to print and advertise her very first book, *Sense and Sensibility*, in 1811.[3]

One of our favorite stories about self-publishing is told by Kate Moore in her book *The Woman They Could Not Silence*.[4] In the 1860s, Elizabeth Packard was wrongly imprisoned in an insane asylum for years. During her time there, she kept copious notes and a detailed journal documenting the atrocities she witnessed. Although she was eventually freed and acquitted, she could not find support with traditional publishers for her memoirs. So she crowd-sourced the funding and self-published them instead! Her advocacy work brought to light many horrors of the insane asylums and she was able to help free many other women.

In fact, self-publishing has played a critical role in toppling corrupt governments and fighting for justice. If you want to rebel against authorities, you're more likely to be able to self-publish your thoughts and opinions than go through mainstream traditional publishers with higher visibility, where you're more likely to be caught—or who would refuse to publish you in the first place. During World War II, the underground press played a major role in the anti-Nazi resistance. Under the USSR, the "samizdat" movement (literally Russian for "self-publishing") arose in defiance of the government's censorship and restrictions on free speech.[5]

Self-publishing has also been a way that historically marginalized authors can have more agency and control over their publishing careers. (Though it shouldn't be this way and in recent years, many in traditional publishing have been working hard to even the playing field and publish more diverse voices.) Poet Rupi Kaur wrote, illustrated, and self-published her debut poetry collection when she was just twenty-one years old. She already had a prominent following on Instagram and used it to sell over eight million copies of both of her *New York Times* best-selling books. She told the *Times of India* that self-publishing gave her the power to overcome her socially marginalized status. "The literary world didn't even see me. I was a 20-year-old, brown, Punjabi Sikh woman from a working class immigrant family," she said.[6] For Kaur, self-publishing meant taking her career into her own hands and not waiting for permission from the traditional gatekeepers.

Rest assured, when you consider the path of self-publishing, you are in *very* good company.

Self-Publishing vs. "Independent" Publishing

Some people prefer the term "independent publishing" to "self-publishing" because it has a better perception and distances authors from the stigma of self-publishing. This can be a bit confusing because in the world of traditional publishing, "independent publishing" refers to publishers outside of the Big 5 who still follow a traditional publishing model, which we'll get to in chapter 15. Using either "self-publishing" or "independent publishing" to refer to the DIY model is perfectly fine; just be sure to clarify what you mean!

How Self-Publishing Works

Self-publishing's answer to the question, "Who bears the most financial risk for this investment (and therefore receives most of the reward)?" is, simply, *you*! With the second question, "Who does which parts of the work?" you have a bit more flexibility. You could do every step of the work yourself, like William Blake did, or you could outsource the work to others who know how to do it, like Jane Austen. You might find freelancers to do each individual piece of the process, or you could hire an assisted self-publishing company to do all of it (except the writing) for you. Either way, though, *you* are responsible for making sure all of the following parts of the process happen:

Mapping and Writing

The first part is the same no matter how you publish. You need to do the foundational work, map your book, and write it.

Editing

Since you will not have an editor at a publishing house assigned to you, we strongly suggest hiring a freelance editor (or two) to take a look at your manuscript before you publish. Your book should go through at least two rounds of editing from a real professional.

Cover Design

Your book cover is the first thing potential readers see. It needs to be visually appealing and relevant to your content. You'll need to invest in a professional cover designer who can create a cover design for you. Take a look at the covers of your comps or bestsellers on Amazon for inspiration. Stick to what others have done in your genre.

Formatting

Formatting is crucial to ensure your book appears polished and readable. You have two primary options:

- DIY Formatting: Use software like Microsoft Word or specialized formatting tools to format your book yourself.
- Professional Formatting: Hire a professional formatter to ensure your book meets industry standards.

When in doubt, hire a professional for this, too. They know what they're doing. And if the formatting of your book turns out wrong, it can make you look like an amateur and degrade the experience for your readers.

ISBN and Copyright

To publish your book, you'll need an ISBN (International Standard Book Number) and consider copyright protection:

- ISBN: Acquire an ISBN, which serves as a unique identifier for your book. Some self-publishing platforms provide free ISBNs.
- Copyright: While your work is automatically copyrighted upon creation, registering it with your country's copyright office adds an extra layer of protection.

Distribution

Now comes the crucial decision: selecting a self-publishing platform. Two of the most popular options are Amazon Kindle Direct Publishing (KDP) and IngramSpark:

- **Amazon KDP:** Ideal for ebooks and print-on-demand (POD) paperbacks, KDP offers a vast audience through the Amazon marketplace.
- **IngramSpark:** Suitable for wider distribution, IngramSpark makes your book available to bookstores, libraries, and online retailers beyond Amazon.

After choosing your platform, follow their specific guidelines for uploading your book. This typically involves uploading your manuscript, cover, and filling out necessary information such as book description, pricing, and keywords.

Marketing

Just like Jane Austen, you will be responsible for making sure your book gets seen by your potential audience!

What about the quality?

One of the biggest objections to self-publishing we hear is that the quality won't be as good as books published through traditional publishing. And it's true that there are a lot of badly self-published books. But that's the beauty of self-publishing: You get to decide on the quality of the final product. It may require more funds, but there are many surprisingly affordable, high-quality printing options available. It just requires a little elbow grease to find them.

Is Self-Publishing Right for You?

Let's talk about a couple of the ways people come to self-publishing. First, you might have been pitching and querying, trying the traditional route for so long that you just feel done. Hear us loud and clear: there is absolutely no shame in this! There are *tons* of reasons why agents or editors might not seem interested in your book proposal that don't have anything to do with how strong your idea is and how much it could impact others. With one quick Google search, you'll find dozens of big names (Tim Ferriss, JK Rowling, Stephen King, Dr. Seuss) who got passed over for book deals many, many times before they eventually landed one. If you have hit your limit with traditional publishing and are ready to take matters into your own hands, that's a great reason to self-publish. Remember, like Rupi Kaur, Hungry Authors don't wait for an invitation to the party; they host their own party if they want to.

Many authors choose self-publishing from day one because there are plenty of benefits to it. Some writers enjoy the control and speed self-publishing allows them. One of the most significant advantages of self-publishing is the complete creative control you have over your work. From cover design to the final edit, you make all the decisions. Traditional publishers often have the final say, which can lead to compromises on your artistic vision. Traditional publishing also takes a long time. It always has, it probably always will. But self-publishing can happen very quickly, within just a few months even, and pretty much depends on how fast you can write your book. You control just about every part of the process. To many authors, this is appealing.

You also receive up to 70 percent of the royalties, meaning you get much more money per book than if you published with a traditional house. Let's say your book is priced at $14.99. For easy math, pretend you were offered a 10 percent royalty structure from a publisher, but if you self-published, you could earn 60 percent of each book. And now let's say in each scenario you sold six thousand books. With the publisher you would make $10,740 and by self-publishing you'd make $34,440. That's a difference of more than $24,000. For many authors, especially those with an established platform and audience, and thus a built-in distribution channel, this is a great option.

Table 14.1 shows a quick summary of the pros and cons of self-publishing.

Table 14.1. Pros and Cons of Self-Publishing

Pros	Cons
• Complete creative control • Speed to market • Higher royalties • Freedom to experiment. You can literally do whatever you want when it comes to self-publishing. For many, this is an advantage.	• Complete responsibility for the production and manufacturing • Initial costs • Stigma. Though this is changing significantly, there is still a level of clout that comes with traditional publishing.

Tips and Tricks

To make the most of self-publishing while mitigating its downsides, consider these tips:

1. Invest in professional services. Budget for professional editing, cover design, and formatting. These services ensure your book meets industry standards.
2. Build an author platform. More on this in chapter 15, but it's just plain harder to get the word out about your book without a publishing house behind you. Having a distribution channel for your books is even more important if you self-publish. Engage with readers and build a community around your work.
3. Learn the business. Take the time to understand the publishing industry, including pricing strategies, genre trends, and marketing techniques.

Hopefully by now we've shown you that self-publishing is a perfectly legitimate and respectable way to produce and disseminate your work. But it still might not be the right choice for you. If you're like many authors we work with, then traditional publishing may have a shimmering appeal. Let's explore this popular publishing pathway.

15

Pitch Your Book
Traditional Publishing

When we ask aspiring authors what their plans are for publishing, almost all of them say they want to traditionally publish their book. And while we're both fans of traditional publishing (we chose to traditionally publish *this* book, after all!), we believe that this preference comes from cultural inertia and the perpetuating myths around both traditional and self-publishing, rather than a thorough understanding of the industry and its pros and cons. Traditional publishing may in fact be the right choice for you, but many authors say they want it without taking the time to thoughtfully consider all of their options. In this chapter, we want to help you get a realistic handle on the traditional pathway for publishing and set you up for success if you decide to pursue it!

How Traditional Publishers Work

The most important thing for you to know about traditional publishing is that traditional publishers are *investors*. Their job is to look for authors, stories, and ideas that a large number of people will want to read and make them widely available to the public in the form of a book. Publishers invest a hefty sum of money for the book to be developed, produced, manufactured in bulk, warehoused, and distributed—and then they hope that it will sell well enough to not only recoup their expenses, but bring in a tidy profit on top. Acquisitions editors are the people responsible for scoping out these possible new investments (i.e., acquisitions) for the company by reviewing book proposals (which we'll talk about in chapter 16).

As you can imagine, the problem acquisitions editors face is that it's incredibly difficult to predict which authors, stories, and ideas will sell well enough for publishers to get a significant return on their investment. Publishers have tried for years to discover a formula or science behind what sells well and what doesn't, but ultimately, there is no formula. Acquisitions editors must rely on a mix of historical data (what has sold well in the past), market trends, and good old-fashioned hunches about what will sell well in order to make their decisions. Unlike products like refrigerators or shoes, where the buyer always knows exactly what to expect and manufacturers can reasonably predict sales based on seasonal market trends, books are a risk for buyers. So much of the buying decision is based on individual buyers' subjective feelings: *Do I like the cover? Is the title intriguing to me? Does it match the "vibe" I want right now? Will it fit in my purse or suitcase? Do my friends like it?* Readers have to take calculated risks based on their individual preferences, and therefore acquisitions editors have to try to guess what vast numbers of readers will want at any point in time.

In 2022, the unpredictability of the publishing industry was put on full display in the federal court case *US vs. Bertelsmann SE & Co. KGaA et al.*—a terrible title for one of the most important events in recent publishing history. Penguin Random House (PRH), at the time the largest publishing company in the United States, owned by Bertelsmann, was attempting to buy Simon & Schuster, the smallest of the "Big 5" publishers. The United States Department of Justice moved to block the acquisition, arguing successfully that it would decrease competition in the publishing industry. The DOJ won their case, and PRH was unable to complete its purchase. But the fascinating trial that unfolded shed light on the inner workings of publishing companies, especially the most successful ones.

In a statement that shocked everyone outside of the publishing industry, then-CEO of Penguin Random House, Markus Dohle, told the court: "Everything is random in publishing. That's why we have that name. So the founder thought: Everything is random. Success is random. Best sellers are random. So that's why we are the Random House."[1] If you're thinking that this doesn't seem like a very reliable business model—you're right.

Joel J. Miller, former vice president of editorial and acquisitions at Thomas Nelson Publishers, writes a popular newsletter called *Miller's Book Review*. He wrote similarly, "Whether at the macro or micro levels, publishing is essentially an institutionalized, intellectual gambling habit with up times and down times."[2] The end goal of both gambling and publishing is always one thing: money. Instead of playing blackjack or craps, though, agents and editors are betting on great authors, great ideas, and great writing.

What Are the Big 5?

The "Big 5" are the five largest publishers in the United States:

- Penguin Random House
- HarperCollins
- Hachette
- Macmillan
- Simon & Schuster

Each of the Big 5 has a number of imprints, or smaller companies that specialize in various genres or topics, within. As of 2022, the Big 5 control about 80 percent of the market share for book publishing.[3] The other 20 percent are comprised of smaller, independent publishers.

Is Traditional Publishing Right for You?

So how do you decide if you want to join this high-stakes game? Remember that the first question every publishing model has to answer is: Who bears the most financial risk for this investment (and therefore receives most of the reward)? In traditional publishing, the answer to this question is "the publisher." They make the greatest financial investment in the project, and they also reap the greatest rewards, in that they will keep most of the profits and pay you an advance (a lump sum of money that you'll need to repay the publisher through your royalties—literally, your royalties in advance) and royalties, after your advance has earned out (typically about 10 percent of the net revenue for first-time authors).

Now let's break down the answer to the second question, Who does which parts of the work?

In a traditional publishing relationship, the author is responsible for:

- Writing the book and responding to feedback from the editorial team
- Turning their draft manuscript in on time
- Cooperating in a timely manner with the rest of the publishing team
- Marketing the book

Hitting your deadlines is incredibly important in traditional publishing because a good portion of publishers' cash flow depends quite literally on when books publish. If you're late, it could cost a publisher tens of thousands of dollars and make them very grumpy. The nice thing is, though, that's really your biggest commitment! Yes, it's still a lot of work, but it's less work than trying to do all of the following tasks yourself, which publishers take on instead:

- Editing and production
- Cover and interior design
- Manufacturing
- Printing
- Contributing to marketing
- Storage and warehousing fees
- Distribution to bookstores
- Managing metadata
- Filing with the Library of Congress
- Assigning an ISBN
- Managing the sales of translations rights (unless your agent is doing that)

Whether this sounds like a good arrangement is highly dependent on the author. Table 15.1 lays out the pros and cons for you more plainly.

Table 15.1. Pros and Cons of Traditional Publishing for Authors

Pros	Cons
• You get to partner with a team of experts • You might get a nice advance when you sign the contract • You benefit from the publisher's name and credibility in the market • Never worry about administrative tasks or hidden costs that arise • Access to a network of distributors to make sure your book is available as widely as possible	• Royalties and advances can be a nice plus, but usually not enough to live on • Publishers retain creative control over the book's cover and title • You are responsible for marketing • The total timeline from proposal to printed book is often eighteen months or more • Often requires a significant author platform • Acceptance depends on a rigorous approval process

Looking at this list, you can decide which factors are most important to you. Maybe it's worth giving up creative control over the cover and title because you trust that these publishing professionals really know their stuff and will give the book its best chance of success. Or maybe you absolutely cannot justify the work it takes to attract a traditional publisher if it's still going to take another year and a half (or more!) to publish. Take some time to think about what's important to you and keep reading to understand what it takes to break into traditional publishing.

What Traditional Publishers Look For

Put yourself in an acquisitions editors' shoes for a minute. You love books—that's why you're here. But the company you work for pays your bills, and the company needs to make money in order for you to keep working on the books you love. So you need to make the company money. You have goals you must reach—usually a set number of titles to acquire, which should bring in a minimum amount of revenue (as best as you can predict). If you want to get promoted and get your bonuses, you can't just bring in the minimum; you've got to find the show-stoppers, the big-ticket books, as well as books that will continue to sell reliably well for many years into the future. You also have a finite amount of money you can offer authors as advances, barring an incredible opportunity magically finding its way across your desk. You're not worried about not being able to find enough authors to meet your goal; agents and authors are constantly banging on the door. The problem is that there are so *many* possible authors. How do you find the best opportunities, the possible *New York Times* bestsellers—especially when every single author whose proposal crosses your desk is convinced that *their* book will be the winner?

Every successful book needs—and therefore every acquisitions editor looks for:

- An audience
- A great idea
- Great writing

If you've been following the advice in this book, then you already have a great idea and a pretty-darn-good draft that will get better with editing. But what about that first point, audience? In chapter 3, we talked about defining who your *potential* readers are. Unfortunately, that's not enough for publishers. They want to know that those readers are, in fact, *already* invested in your book and what you have to offer. This is what the publishing industry means when they talk about that dreaded word "platform."

The Truth about Platform

You can't get anywhere far in pursuit of traditional publishing before you run into the term "platform," usually placed like a big brick wall in-between authors and their dreams. Typically, platform is reduced to mere numbers—and social media numbers, at that. You'll hear authors and publishing industry insiders alike spouting numbers like, "You need one hundred thousand followers to get a book deal," or "You need ten thousand newsletter subscribers to get a book deal." Everyone seems to have a different number—and all of them either make prospective authors (who don't have those numbers) feel like failures *or* offer prospective authors (who do have those numbers) a false sense of security, as if a book deal is guaranteed. The emphasis on platform is so overblown that most people forget that, in fact, you *do* need those other two components of a great idea and great writing—and, as you'll see, sometimes it's still just not a good fit for a publisher, for legitimate reasons that have nothing to do with the author or the book. On the other hand, many authors with little to no social media following achieve traditional publishing success all the time.

To prove it, let's take a look at a small selection of *New York Times* nonfiction bestsellers from July and August 2023 and their authors' social media followings as of that time in table 15.2. Whenever you're reading this, feel free to peruse the current *NYT* list and do your own analysis. Yes, the celebrities and high-profile influencers will be there, too—but you'll be surprised at what you find!

Table 15.2. *New York Times* Best-selling Authors' Social Media Followers

Title	Author	Number of Social Media Followers (as of August 2023)
The Book of Charlie	David von Drehle	3,522 on Instagram
What an Owl Knows	Jennifer Ackerman	2,947 on Instagram
Poverty, By America	Matthew Desmond	37,400 on Twitter
The Underworld	Susan Casey	1,900 on Facebook 3,598 on Instagram
The Fourth Turning Is Here	Neil Howe	39,200 on Twitter

Three of these books' authors have audiences of less than six thousand; two have less than fifty thousand—all still firmly in the category of "small" social media followings. And yet these authors have achieved what many consider to be the pinnacle of publishing success.

So forget about the myths and misconceptions you've heard about platform. Let's get to the truth.

Platform Is More Than Just Social Media

Your platform is the collection of possible avenues you have for reaching readers of your potential audience. Platform is a set of tools that goes well beyond just social media. It includes social media *and* . . .

- Your email newsletter list
- Your website/app viewers and users
- Any organizations you are part of that serve your audience
- The other influential people you are connected to, who would promote your book to their audiences
- Speaking engagements and consulting business
- Articles you've written in both large and small publications online

Platform Expectations Differ by Genre

Remember back to chapter 2: Genre determines most everything else about your book—including, perhaps surprisingly, the author platform that readers will expect.

For self-help and other prescriptive nonfiction genres, readers expect that the author will have significant credibility and expertise on their topic; that's why they're qualified to give others advice. No one wants to read a book about proper nutrition from someone who's never studied nutrition. Not only do you have to have the credentials, though; you also have to show publishers that people actively look to you as an authority on that topic. That means you probably speak on that topic at conferences or give workshops. Ideally, you are an "influencer" on social media on that topic and you cultivate a thriving email list of people who look forward to the advice you send out on your topic. Prescriptive nonfiction authors are held to the highest platform standards.

For creative nonfiction genres, the platform requirements are often much lower. Readers don't expect that memoir writers will necessarily have a massive platform; they simply don't need to. Remember in chapter 2 we shared Jane Friedman's analysis of authors who were signed for memoir deals in 2022. Her big finding was that, contrary to popular belief, you do *not* need to be a celebrity to write a memoir! Anyone can come from any life background and have an incredible story to tell—that's part of what makes memoir so fun to read. Narrative nonfiction is the same. When it comes to social media in particular, many best-selling memoir and narrative nonfiction authors often have a small presence or no presence whatsoever.

Platform Expectations Differ by Publisher

The "Big 5"—that is, the five largest publishers in the United States, all owned by larger media or private equity companies—usually expect their nonfiction authors to come with a "large" platform. While, again, numbers differ based on who you ask, typically they are looking for authors with tens of thousands if not hundreds of thousands of readers, through their social media and/or through bylines, speaking engagements, and so on. That doesn't, however, mean that an acquisitions editor at a Big 5 publisher or one of their imprints won't sign an author with a much smaller platform; it happens all the time. It just means that there will be significant barriers and that those authors will likely hear many more "nos" before they hear a "yes."

Smaller independent, niche publishers are often more amenable to authors with small platforms. They often care more about the authors' credibility and associations than stark numbers.

You Need an Audience, But It Doesn't Have to Be *Your* Audience

During the first year of the pandemic, sales for books on distance learning skyrocketed as students transitioned to doing school at home with their families. Books about politics always do better during a heated election period. Obviously, you can't always predict events like this. But you *can* find topics and subjects that have large followings and that are uniquely relevant to the times.

Author Catherine Baab-Muguira used this principle to great success with her first book, *Poe for Your Problems: Uncommon Advice from History's Least Likely Self-Help Guru.* She writes:

> When I sold my nonfiction debut back in 2019, I had the same modest following that I do now: a few thousand on Twitter, and effectively none on Facebook, Instagram, or YouTube. The way I made my case was by focusing on my *subject's* platform instead. I wanted to write a book about Edgar Allan Poe, so in my book proposal, I spent a great deal of time outlining Poe's platform, both his online following and its physical, meat-world manifestations.
>
> Sure, the guy has been dead for almost 200 years, and still he has 3.6 million Facebook fans—more than James Patterson or Danielle Steele. . . . If I were a marquee-name writer with a track record of bestsellers, I wouldn't have a bigger platform than Poe.[4]

This brilliant strategy led to a book deal, and Cat has been teaching other prospective authors to use the same strategy ever since. She writes that you can find similar ready-to-buy audiences all around you! Just look for the groups on Facebook, the communities on Reddit, or the people asking fervent questions on Quora. Start paying attention to what interests people around you, and you might stumble on an audience that's just waiting for the book you're going to write.

There Is No Magic Number

Ten thousand, one hundred thousand—there's no consensus on the "right" number because there is none. Bigger is always better, but even a "big" platform is no guarantee that a book will sell to publishers, or that, once published, it will sell well.

Just ask Billie Eilish and Justin Timberlake, both of whom have millions of followers across social media platforms and whose books did not meet sales expectations.[5] These instances, and many more besides, are just proof that the number of people following you doesn't necessarily translate into real sales. It's very easy to get someone to tap "follow" on social media—but it's very hard to get that person to spend twenty to thirty dollars on a nine- or ten-hour time commitment without a better reason than just "I think they're cool."

Every Publishing Professional Thinks about Platform Differently

We've met agents who say "platform doesn't matter," and we've met agents who say, "Don't talk to me unless you have one hundred thousand people on your email list." The only truth about platform is that no one quite agrees on how valuable or necessary it is to your publishing success.

We take all of this as very good news. Yes, if you decide to pitch a proposal and you don't have gajillions of followers, you'll likely hear "small platform" as a reason for rejection at some point. But hopefully you see that it's still worth it to try; you'll just have to work harder to make your idea, your credibility, and your writing as strong as possible, and find the right fit for you and your book.

How to Pitch Traditional Publishers

If you've read this far and you still want to make a go at traditional publishing, that's great! Let's talk about your next steps.

First, you'll need a book proposal. You can think of your book proposal like a business plan. Imagine that you were applying to a bank for a small business loan to get a business started. You would need to come up with a business plan to show the bank how you plan on making the business successful so that you can repay their loan (with interest). Publishing operates similarly. Since publishers are, essentially, investors, they want to see that you have a strong plan to make the book successful so that they will recoup their investment in you and your idea. In chapter 16, we'll share our best tips and insights for creating a convincing plan for your book's success!

The next thing you'll need is a great query letter. Also sometimes called a cover letter, this "letter" (usually an email nowadays!) introduces agents and publishers to your book idea and is used to invite them to read your whole proposal. Query letters are ideally short, direct, and engaging—your goal is to convince the reader (i.e., the agent or publisher) to peruse your book proposal in as few words as possible (typically about 250–400).

When you've got your documents ready, you'll need to strategize about which publishers you want to target for your proposal. Depending on who your audience is and the size of that audience, you may want to pitch academic or professional publishers directly. Often these independent, niche presses accept submissions directly from authors and don't require the intermediary of an agent. Do your research and make sure that they already publish books like yours. Don't send a poetry book to a small textbook publisher, or a memoir to a business publisher; they're not going to say yes to those queries, not because your idea or writing is bad but because it's just not a good fit for them. Take the time to find the right publishers that publish books in your genre and topic area before you pitch them.

Many publishers, including Big 5 and larger trade publishers, require that authors have representation by a literary agent, who will submit their proposal to the publisher on the authors' behalf. Literary agents are intermediaries; their job is both to act as a frontline curator of proposals for publishers, and to advocate for authors throughout the publishing process. Great literary agents form close, long-term relationships with their authors, acting as their concierge to the publishing world, which, as you might guess, can be quite a confusing place! They will negotiate better advances and contract terms for you, help you understand the legal lingo in a contract, and liaise between the publisher whenever something goes awry. Agents are reimbursed when a publishing deal is signed, usually with a 15 to 20 percent cut of your advance and royalties. While this might sound like a high cost, in most cases, it is completely worth it and we highly encourage authors to enlist the help of a reputable agent in securing a publishing deal.

The process of finding an agent is similar to finding a publisher: You'll email them your query letter (in the body of the email)—unless their website specifically requests a different submissions process—and invite them to read your full proposal. If they say yes and like your proposal, then you'll likely have a meeting with them to learn more about the support they provide for authors and determine whether you both like each other. It's a little like dating!

So how do you find the right agents to pitch? Like publishers, most agents specialize in a few favorite genres, be it business and professional books, health and wellness, or memoirs. Here are our favorite tips for finding the most likely agents to pitch:

- Look at the acknowledgments sections in your comp titles. Hopefully, the authors have thanked their literary agents by name. These are good agents to pitch, since they've already demonstrated that they're interested in the same genre/topic and have a track record of success securing book deals.
- Subscribe to Publishers Marketplace. While this has a monthly or annual cost, it is worth it for the incredible access you get to a database of publishing professionals' contact information. Search for your topic to find other similar books and see which agents represent them. Add those agents to your list.

- Google "literary agent + [your topic/genre]." Yes, we really do this, and yes, it really works. Literary agents *want* to be found by great potential authors, so even though they are inundated with requests, their websites and contact information are usually easily found online!
- Search manuscriptwishlist.com. As the name suggests, this site exists to help agents find proposals on their "wishlist." While most agents on the site are dedicated to fiction, many are also looking for nonfiction titles as well. Search the site for your topic to find agents who might be a good match!

Q&A

Q: How many agents should I pitch?
A: Pitch in batches! Find ten to twenty likely agents that you'd like to pitch first. Send them your query letter, and then wait three to four weeks for responses. If you don't hear back, feel free to send them ONE friendly nudge to make sure they received your query. If you still don't hear back, or if you receive all "nos," move on and pitch another ten to twenty agents. Repeat the process until you find your "yes" or decide that it's not worth it to continue. In which case, head back to chapter 14!

Q: How long should I keep pitching?
A: Only you can determine how long you should keep pitching. We recommend setting an overall end limit for yourself, depending on what feels reasonable and sustainable to you ("I'm going to pitch two hundred agents" or "I'm going to try pitching ten to twenty agents every month for six months"). Pitching is hard work, and it can be emotionally draining to receive rejections. If you find that your enthusiasm for your book is waning, it may be time to move on to chapter 14.

Make sure that as you find agents, you read their websites, biographies, and descriptions thoroughly to make sure both that you are the right fit for them, and that they are the right fit for you. While most authors often feel desperate for an agent to say "yes" to them, that doesn't necessarily mean they'll be the best advocate for your work. Unfortunately, there are many people out there who will prey on authors' desperation (as we'll discuss more in chapters 16 and 17!), including some literary agents. Beware of agents who charge a fee to read or edit your proposal.

Grow from the Rejections

No matter what path to traditional publishing you take, it's almost guaranteed that you *will* encounter rejection. Rejection is a rite of passage for authors and should never be a reason to stop pitching or believing in your book. In many cases, you'll simply not hear back—sometimes for days, weeks, months, or ever. Many of the rejections you receive will be bland and generic: "This isn't a good fit for my list," or "I'm not taking on projects on this topic at the moment." Occasionally, you'll receive a rejection that is specific to your book: "I didn't connect with the writing samples," or "Your platform is too small for my list," or "I love the idea but I just haven't had luck selling books like yours in the past." Always, *always* thank an agent (or publisher) for taking the time to respond to you. You can also try asking them (very politely, and only once) what you might do to improve the proposal before you submit it to someone else. The worst they can do is not respond!

If an agent or publisher responds with specific advice about how you can improve your pitch or proposal, take it seriously. You may or may not want to take their advice. For example, they might say, "Memoirs about mental health aren't selling right now, but if you reposition it as a self-help book guiding readers through depression, I'd be interested."

At that point, you have a choice to make, and you know by now that changing the genre of a book is no simple matter. You cannot just slap some reflection questions on the end of each chapter and call it self-help. The Transformation Tale for a self-help book will look radically different from what you planned for your memoir, so you'll need to think carefully about whether you want to make those kinds of massive changes. Remember to go back to your "why" and ask yourself what your goals are. For some authors, switching to self-help might be just the thing; for others, it might feel like an abandonment of self. This is *your* book. It has to be something you love and believe in.

If, on the other hand, what the agent/publisher suggests is an easy change and doesn't require a compromise in your vision for the project, then you have nothing to lose and everything to gain by taking their advice and implementing it immediately. Maybe it is worth it to spend the next three to six months growing your Substack subscribers before continuing to pitch. They might not necessarily be interested in looking at the proposal again once you make that change (though you should ask!), but you can rest assured that their suggestion will increase your odds of success with someone else.

Remember this: Agents and publishers *want* to work with great authors whose projects will be both personally and financially rewarding. Most publishing professionals you meet are book people—who, you probably know, are the best people in the world. They love reading, they love great ideas, and they love supporting authors. Stay positive and have faith that if you believe in your book, someone else will, too.

On that note, let's teach you how to write the book proposal that will knock their socks off!

16

Create a Book Proposal

Let's return to Brittany Estes from the introduction for a moment. Brittany landed an agent and a book deal quickly for a number of reasons that we already covered. First and foremost, she was a Hungry Author. She was always going to succeed no matter what. Secondly, she had a plan. She knew what she wanted to write about and how she was going to execute her book and publishing path. For her, that chosen path was traditional publishing. For that, she needed a stellar book proposal.

Brittany did a lot of things right in her proposal. She had a solid foundation, like we talked about in part I. She had a great idea and a unique angle, understood her audience, and knew where her book fit into the marketplace. Because of this she was able to accomplish the two most important things a book proposal do:

1. Make a business case for your book.
2. Not just talk about it, but communicate the urgent need for it.

Let's discuss the first. One of the most misunderstood things about book proposals is that they are first and foremost, a business document. A book proposal is a pitch to agents and editors about why your book will sell well. It should not be about how amazing your idea is and how much you love it and how passionate you are about it. (Although it will include some of that, and I'm sure you are.) Here's a little tough love: agents and editors don't care much about that. Or at least they don't care about that the *most*.

Like we discussed in chapter 15, publishing is a business like any other industry. Editors, agents, and publishing houses want to make money so they can stay in business and keep their jobs. Fair enough, right? The way they do that is by publishing books that they believe will sell well enough to make them that money. If industry experts pick enough authors and books that do not sell commercially well, they will lose their jobs, just like in any other career.

So your mindset when writing a book proposal should be that you are making a case that this book will be a successful investment. Remember, publishing is a risk-averse industry. They like safe bets.

We want you to view yourself as the answer to a problem agents and editors have. They are constantly looking for new talent. They want to find Hungry Authors who are determined to succeed no matter what, and who will be equal partners in this endeavor to bring the book to market. Many first-time authors see agents and editors as the gatekeepers to their dreams. But when you write your proposal, we want you to see yourself as exactly what they've been looking for. An equal partner who can help them get what they want (to make money working on books they're excited about) as they help you get what you want (to be a published author).

The second thing a book proposal absolutely must do (and a huge mistake first-time authors make when they do the inverse) is not focus entirely on the content but on why the book matters right now for this audience. Don't write so much about what your book is *about,* but why it is *urgently needed.* Even though you are writing about a timeless topic, you need to make it clear that your unique solution to a problem, point of view, new information, recently discovered data, and so on is relevant to the market today. Creative nonfiction authors, the same applies to you, too, although it can be harder to make the case when your book isn't as straightforward as problem-solution. Remember, you are still walking the protagonist and reader through a transformation. How is that relevant to your target audience? What difference will it make in their life? You might have to lean a little harder on your Comp Title Analysis here to prove a market for your book. More on that in a minute.

Here's a quick primer on the basics of book proposals. While they vary greatly in length, most are at least thirty pages, and some can be upwards of fifty, including the sample chapters. For this book, ours was sixty-six. All book proposals are different. Like many things in the publishing industry, there is no one right way to do it. Every writer, editor, agent, or book coach has their own preferred style and template. But there are certain sections that all book proposals must include to succeed. Those are an Overview, Author Bio, Target Audience, Comp Title Analysis, Market Analysis/Positioning, Marketing Plan/Promotion, Outline/Chapter Summaries, and Sample Chapters.

Let's dig into these.

Overview

The Overview is almost always at the beginning of your proposal. Essentially, it is a summary of what your book is about, who it serves, why the world needs it now, and why you are the one to write it. Be sure to include the overall transformation your book delivers for its readers. Overviews need to be concise and not overly lengthy. Don't prognosticate. It should be around two to three pages. Though it can be helpful to have a working version of the Overview when you start your proposal to guide the writing and thinking throughout the rest of it, you'll almost always have to return and revise it as your idea sharpens and evolves.

It's a good idea to start your first sentence strong with either an anecdotal lead (like a story), a starting statistic, or a bold statement. You have no room to spare and no time to waste in book proposals. Get right to the point. Below is an easy template to follow when writing an Overview.

Overview Template

Hook:
- [Interesting story or anecdote]
- [Compelling question]
- [Surprising data]
- [Reader interaction]
- [Analogy]

Every [YOUR READER] wants . . .

The problem is . . .
- What gets in the way of getting what they want?
- What catalyst is disrupting their life?
- Why are they having that problem?
- How does that problem make them feel?
- How do they deny the situation or make it worse?
- What does it cost them?

The solution is . . .
- What will the hero know/think/do differently by the end of the book?
- What happens as a result of this transformation?

To give you an example of this in action, here was our original Overview for this book:

Overview

Every aspiring writer knows how it feels to have something important to say—a message burning in their veins. They know the next step is immortalizing it in a book. They feel passionate and invigorated, ready to take action.

So they type "How do I publish a book?" into a search engine and learn two things right away: One, writing a book is hard. Two, their chances of publishing success are low. As they dig deeper, the results overwhelm, confuse, and discourage them. Sometimes the information on page one contradicts the information on page two. Plus, the persistent "scarcity narrative" around publishing clangs in the minds of hopeful writers, making them feel like the publishing world is some kind of exclusive club—and they don't have the right connections to even get in the door. Exasperated, they think, I want to create a high-quality book that impacts the world, but this seems impossible!

It's time to flip the script. We believe any author with a great idea can write and publish a kick-ass book. We'll help them do this by:

- *encouraging them to establish the right mindset,*
- *coaching them to create a solid plan,*
- *guiding them through the writing process, and*
- *teaching them how to pitch and publish their book.*

It's not easy; it takes grit, gumption, and a stick-with-it-ness that keeps them committed to the work despite all obstacles. But if you've got the hunger and the know-how, it can be done. We see it every day and know that the difference between authors who make it and authors who don't is not platform—the usual scapegoat for books that die on the vine—but mindset and a solid plan. Aspiring authors don't have to wait to be invited to an exclusive club; they can crash the party or make their own. We'll show these Hungry Authors the broad spectrum of publishing opportunities, and our insider knowledge will allow writers to confidently submit their work to agents and editors—or help them decide if hybrid or self-publishing are their best options. There are so many publishing possibilities available, if only they will try.

Hungry Authors have an important message and story that the world needs, and we want to help them share it. We want to take them from desperation to determination, from overwhelm to focus, and from confusion to clarity. Their hunger isn't a liability; it's an asset. We can give authors an outlet for their energy and message to the benefit of the industry as a whole.

Author Bio

Your Author Bio is more than just your résumé or the bio on your website or LinkedIn. In a proposal, your bio also has to show why you are the perfect author for this book. Start with those of your credentials that explain most clearly why you are highly qualified to teach about your topic. Explain how your expertise and experience makes you the right person to write this book for this audience. Include relevant pieces of your personal story, as well. If you want to include unrelated professional credentials, put them near the bottom. You can find ours at the back of this book. It's also a good idea to include a professional headshot here.

Target Audience

We covered target audience in chapter 3 so that comes into play again here. Who is the most likely readership of your book? Who will be digitally lining up to preorder and help get the word out? You'll want to address those psychographics and demographics that we discussed earlier. Consider gender, age, professional status, as well as their internal struggles and desires. Add in as much hard data as you can. You want to quantify the number of people in your target audience as much as possible.

Here is our original target audience from our proposal:

Target Audience

This book is for aspiring nonfiction writers, ages 20–45, who are ready to get published. We are especially writing for young entrepreneurs, influencers, activists, difference-makers, change-agents, and for anyone else who feels like their message is too big to hold back any longer. These would-be authors have big goals but aren't yet making more than $100,000. They still have a small platform, but they're actively taking steps to grow it—and they'll stop at nothing to be successful.

These authors are tired of hearing the publishing odds are stacked against them, and they're looking for an actionable, hopeful guide. They know that they are meant to write and publish their books, and are determined to find a way. In short, this book is for all the Hungry Authors out there who are going places—no matter how they publish. As for us, we're going with them.

BONUS. It can be a great idea to include a Features and Benefits section here that covers what exactly your book will do for this specific audience. Like the one we did for our book.

Features and Benefits:

This book offers aspiring nonfiction authors:
- *Hope and optimism about the publishing landscape*
- *A fresh and humorous perspective on the work and business of being a writer*
- *A practical roadmap for ideating, planning, writing, and publishing their book*
- *Pragmatic advice for determining the best publishing path for them*
- *Insider wisdom and instruction on how to write a book that connects with an audience*
- *Tips and tricks for how to get an agent or publisher's attention, even without a huge platform*

Market Analysis/Positioning

Hey hey, we're circling back again. Aren't you pleasantly surprised that you already have the answers to so many of these questions?! Since we worked on positioning in chapter 4, here is where you get to show off how much you know about the publishing landscape and what your book uniquely offers it, especially in relation to other titles out there.

Here is our positioning paragraph from our book proposal:

Positioning

Books about writing and publishing are like lightning bugs in June—they're everywhere. Many are self-published, and a number of worthy titles are traditionally published. They all offer fairly helpful advice from a variety of perspectives: bestselling authors, publishing professionals, accomplished agents, and loquacious teachers. Most of these books either take a broad brush approach to covering all aspects of the publishing industry for writers of every genre, or they focus specifically on the craft of writing or the business of launching a book. Our book lives somewhere in the middle; we aim to help aspiring nonfiction authors define their unique idea, map out their book, write it, and pursue the right-for-them path to publishing.

We're also returning to our beloved comp titles again as part of analyzing the marketplace. See? You'll need them in many stages of your publishing journey. You'll need to include a section called Comparative/Competitive Title Analysis. Though there's a good chance many of your comp titles that you used to model your structure will apply here, some might not, and you are welcome to choose other books that you didn't examine in mapping. This section typically includes five to ten titles, ideally written within the last five years. We recommend not using books published more than ten years ago. They should have over five hundred reviews on Amazon (indicates good sales) and not be self-published unless you are

204 / Chapter 16

sure it was an absolute, knock-out success (like Hal Elrod's *Miracle Morning* or *Can't Hurt Me* by David Goggins). For each comp, note the title, subtitle, author, publisher, the publisher, and ISBN number. Then for each book, briefly summarize its approach to the topic in relation to your own angle. Basically, how your book is like that particular competing title and how it is different. Write about one to two hundred words for each book.

A word of advice here: do not say anything negative about the books. You do not know the opinions of the editors and agents who will see your proposal, and if they really like a competing title that you trash, you may instantly disqualify yourself. Worse yet, they might have even worked on that book or know the author. Keep it professional and simply say how your book is similar and different, and make the case that there is an audience for your book because of the audience for these books.

Creative nonfiction writers, if you find your audience or positioning hard to describe, you can often make the best case for your book here. If there are other books similar to yours that have sold well, that alone can be a fantastic argument for acquisition.

Here is an example from our Comp Title Analysis:

Before and After the Book Deal: A Writer's Guide to Finishing, Publishing, Promoting, and Surviving Your First Book by Courtney Maum; Catapult; January 2020; ISBN: 978-1948226400

This edited book is a compendium of advice from over 150 contributors across the book industry, including authors, agents, publishers, publicists, and more. It's compiled in a Q&A format, spanning all genres and phases of writing and publishing. It takes a very broad approach to helping authors understand nearly every facet of the industry, aiming to answer every possible question any writer could ever have. It's comprehensive, but at over 350 pages, it is best used as a reference guide when writers have specific questions. Our book, in contrast, is meant to be read start to finish and focuses more narrowly on helping nonfiction writers through the developmental stages of their book and preparing them to publish.

Marketing Plan/Promotion

This is where you will discuss how you plan to promote and distribute your book. Yes, it involves the dreaded "p" word. Platform, in the context of trying to write and sell your book, is essentially your distribution channel. Remember, it's simply the collection of possible avenues you have for reaching readers of your potential audience. Who do you have access to? Who already knows about you? Who will help you promote it? What do you plan to do to get your book in front of the eyes of as many people as possible? Here are some examples of what you should mention in this section:

- Social media, email list numbers, and website hits.
- Influential connections you might have that are willing to promote and endorse the book.
- Podcasts you have/can go on, local news stations, YouTube channels, print or digital publications that will feature you, and so on.
- Speaking engagements.
- Ads or any kind of paid marketing campaigns.
- Members and agencies you belong to.
- Any programs or courses you run, or paid offerings you have.
- What you could potentially do to stir up excitement for the launch. Include any bonuses for preorders, live events, or book tour plans.

We haven't included the Hungry Authors marketing section here because it's way too long. With the exception of your sample chapters, this should be your longest section. Publishers want to know that you will be an equal partner in promoting the book. Show them that you know how important it is to be a mouthpiece and that you won't rely on them entirely to do this work. One of the most important things to keep in mind here is to not only discuss all the ideas you have for how you will market in the future, but the readership and reach you already have right now. (And if you don't have one . . . you should get working on one.) It's easy to promise that you'll do all kinds of grand things on launch day. But what is much more convincing is what you have already done and are doing right now.

Chapter Summaries/Outline/ Annotated Table of Contents

More great news, because of your mapping. You basically already have this! For each chapter, write a brief summary of what that chapter is about, including the little transformation that your reader or self/protagonist will undergo. You can include any stories that will be central to the chapter, main ideas, practical takeaways, exercises, or anything that makes the chapter stand out. Your entire chapter outline shouldn't be more than about three thousand words.

Here is an example of one chapter summary from our proposal:

Chapter 2. Define Your Audience

A successful book by any measure begins with knowing who you're writing for. In this chapter we'll walk aspiring authors through how to define their audience, both demographically and psychographically. How old are they? What are their professions? What are their daily struggles? What do they worry about? Identifying the audience for your book clarifies every part of the process that comes next and serves as a filter for future decisions about what to include.

You might notice that once we got started writing our book, we moved the order of chapters in part I around a bit, so that the chapter on audience (originally intended to be chapter 2) became chapter 3!

Sample Chapters

If you have already written your book following all our advice in part III, then you already have this done as well. It's common for book proposals to include two to three chapters usually not surpassing more than ten thousand words total. If you are writing creative nonfiction, it's best to include the first few chapters of your book. This is a great idea for prescriptive nonfiction too, though not mandatory. For prescriptive, we advise that you submit your most impressive chapters, those that you are proudest of. Choose the ones you think make the best first impression.

Memoir and narrative writers, you need to really shine here. Of course, every author wants their sample chapters to be great, but it's a fact of the industry that the quality of writing matters more for narrative books. Take your time. Study storytelling principles or take a course. It's worth it to make sure your writing truly sings. There's no need for us to share our sample chapters here because you've basically just read them.

Writing a book proposal is a magnum opus, but if you've done the foundational work throughout the rest of this book, it should come easy-ish to you. Remember, we know how much you love your precious book baby, but your proposal is not the place for that kind of talk. It's the place to be an advocate for how salable and marketable your book is in today's market. Now, if you don't want to traditionally publish, or you've tried and things haven't gone your way, do not fret, friend. You already know about the possible benefits waiting for you in self-publishing. But there's one more publishing model that shouldn't be missed when you're exploring all of your options: hybrid publishing.

17

Partner for Success

Hybrid Publishing

Reading the last few chapters, you may have found yourself thinking, "Surely there's a middle ground between these two publishing extremes!" Wouldn't it be great if there was some way to get the credibility and production help of traditional publishing *and* the higher royalties of self-publishing, all rolled into one? There is! That's the idea and the promise of hybrid publishing.

How Hybrid Publishers Work

Publishing is an industry poised for innovation, and in recent decades many publishing professionals and ambitious entre-preneurs have set about experimenting with a third business model that allows for profit sharing with authors. In other words, these "hybrid" publishers take a different approach to publishing: Let's invest in this project *together*, and split the profits.

Many authors don't want to take on the risk and task management inherent in self-publishing, but for whatever reason they have not received a "yes" from traditional publishers or don't want to pursue traditional publishing either. Hybrid publishers take on all of the administrative, production, manufacturing, and distribution tasks of traditional publishers, but the author helps to offset the costs for these tasks so that the publisher alone isn't bearing all of the risk if the book doesn't sell once it's published. Typically, authors will pay between ten and fifty thousand dollars or more to the publisher as their contribution to the investment of the book. Authors' royalties, then, are usually about 50 percent, but may fall anywhere in the range of 40 to 60 percent. Often, hybrid publishers will also provide a suite of à la carte additional services like coaching, developmental editing, marketing, or publicity as optional upgrades to their publishing plan.

Hybrid publishers differ from assisted self-publishing services in a few key ways. Most crucially, hybrids are not a pay-to-play service; instead, they employ highly experienced acquisitions editors that cultivate a list of books in a certain market area, just as editors do at traditional publishers. Authors must still submit book proposals, although the gatekeeping in hybrid publishing is not quite as stringent as it is in the traditional model, since by definition publishers are risking *less* in the hybrid model (they're still risking some!). Hybrid publishers also commit to meeting industry standards for the quality of the books they publish and provide the same level of distribution as traditional publishers. Truly, the only difference between traditional publishers and hybrids is that authors share the initial investment *and* the profits of the book.

The Independent Book Publishers Association (IBPA) is a not-for-profit organization that provides advocacy, education, and tools for the independent publishing community. To help authors understand the role of hybrid publishers, the IBPA has created a list of eleven criteria for hybrid publishers to meet. According to these standards, a hybrid publisher must:

1. Define a mission and vision for its publishing program.
2. Vet submissions.
3. Commit to truth and transparency in business practices.
4. Provide a negotiable, easy-to-understand contract for each book published.
5. Publish under its own imprint and ISBNs.
6. Publish to industry standards.
7. Ensure editorial, design, and production quality.
8. Pursue and manage a range of publishing rights.
9. Provide distribution services.
10. Demonstrate respectable sales.
11. Pay authors a higher-than-standard royalty.[1] (Used with permission from IBPA, 2022)

If you're interested in this publishing model as an author, you'll want to make sure that any company you explore partnering with meets all these criteria.

Is Hybrid Publishing Right for You?

Hybrid publishing can be an attractive option for many authors; in fact, we considered pursuing it ourselves! We've known many authors who have published with hybrids and enjoyed the experience. Table 17.1 lists the possible pros and cons of this arrangement, to help you make the best decision for yourself and your book.

If you find yourself persuaded by the possible benefits of hybrid publishing, then you should make sure you know where and how to find good hybrids with a solid track record and excellent reputation.

Table 17.1. Pros and Cons of Hybrid Publishing for Authors

Pros	Cons
• You get to partner with a team of experts • You benefit from the publisher's name and credibility in the market • Never worry about administrative tasks or hidden costs that arise • Access to a network of distributors to make sure your book is available as widely as possible • Higher royalties (usually 40–60 percent) than traditional publishing • More creative control around the cover and interior design • Option to pay for additional marketing/publicity support • No need of a literary agent to represent you (although they can!)	• Higher possibility of scams • You make an upfront payment to help cover publisher's costs • You are responsible for marketing • The total timeline from proposal to printed book is often eighteen months or more • Requires a book proposal

How to Find Reputable Hybrid Publishers

Hybrid publishing is intended to be the best of both worlds—the creative control and higher profits of self-publishing, combined with the production and distribution power of traditional publishing. But although the IBPA criteria provide a helpful guideline for authors and publishers, there's no official oversight or regulation to ensure good, ethical business practices. This is the Wild West of publishing, and unfortunately, scams abound. Some companies market themselves as "hybrid publishers" and reach out directly to authors to market their "services." Authors are often thrilled, too—*a publisher is reaching out to ME?* It's every author's dream!

If this happens to you, you can feel good about the compliment, but do make sure that the company is a legitimate publisher. Yes, they might see something in you—but hopefully what they see is more than just an easy victim. If anyone claiming to be in the publishing industry makes one of these promises to you, it's worth doing more research to ensure they're legit:

- We'll publish your book in X (insanely short) time period!
- Your book will receive an award.
- We'll market your book to Hollywood for a film adaptation.
- We'll get your book into any bookstore anywhere in the country/world.
- We'll provide X marketing services (like press releases, email campaigns, social media, etc.).

Sure, these promises all sound amazing; but they might be too good to be true. No matter what publisher you consider, we recommend contacting other authors who have worked with them before and who may be able to vouch for them, asking for any proof they can provide of their claims, and ordering a couple books they've published so that you can verify for yourself the quality of the production. A real publisher will have no problem providing these assurances. You may also want to seek out a lawyer who specializes in publishing contracts to double check that the terms they are offering you are indeed favorable and help you understand the risks you might incur if something does go wrong. In fact, this is good practice, no matter what publishing model you decide to pursue! The Authors Guild is another nonprofit that offers advocacy and support for authors. They have a team of lawyers on staff who can help members understand and negotiate contracts and avoid scams. Finally, the blog Writer Beware keeps an up-to-date list of known publishing scams that you can check if you're worried that a company might be a hoax.

Remember that there's no right or wrong way to publish your book. If you decide to go one route and discover that you don't like it, there's nothing stopping you from choosing a different route for your next book. This book is preparation for the next one. All of us are continuing to learn and grow in our journey as Hungry Authors.

Conclusion

The World Is Waiting

A few years ago, two Internet acquaintances became real friends because of one shared goal: they wanted to write a book. They didn't have a big platform, endless money to spend, a big city address, or recognizable names. They were also writing about a very saturated topic: writing. But none of that mattered. What they did have was an idea, a message, some expertise, a plan, and a lot of determination.

From the beginning, they set out to hybrid or self-publish. They loved the idea of having creative control and getting their book out fast. They could hardly wait to see it in the hands of their readers and believed their message was needed urgently. And then one day, early in the writing process, they wondered aloud if they should shoot their shot with traditional publishing. They were experienced writers, after all. Maybe a publisher would bite. So they wrote a book proposal, found an agent who shared their excitement, and were on their way.

Despite being first-time authors, they did have a few publishing connections, so they tapped those early. But it didn't make a difference. They did rounds and rounds of submissions for their book proposal and only heard "no." Just as often, they heard nothing at all. Dead silence as they sent their life's dream out into cyberspace to see if anybody else liked it. Eventually, it had been six months and over twenty rejections. One day during their weekly Friday call they decided, "Oh well. We tried. Let's do it ourselves. That was the plan from the beginning, anyway." Admittedly, they were a little disappointed. Rejection never feels good, and writing and submitting a book proposal is a huge undertaking. But it had taken enough time away from their goal and it was time to get back to business: writing a book. Getting it out into the world was what really mattered and they didn't care how it happened.

Then, on a random Friday in April, came an email from a publisher. *We'd love to talk with you about publishing your book.* The friends enthusiastically took the call with an independent publisher in Washington, DC, and soon enough signed their first book deal. It was a dream come true. Their message would soon be out in the world in the hands and hearts of other would-be authors. It's what every writer wishes for.

AND. It was not made possible because a traditional publisher eventually said yes. It was not possible because a publishing connection let them in the door (they didn't) or because their idea was so irresistible nobody could pass it up (plenty did) or because they had thousands of readers (they didn't). It happened because it was *always* going to happen. The only secret ingredient here is that no one was going to stop us. Oh, yeah. This was us. That is the story of the book in your hands. We are the Hungry Authors who made it happen.

We know the power of Hungry Authorship because we have lived it. There will be tremendous ups and downs in your journey to writing and publishing a book. You will get an idea that you think is genius only to try it on the page and realize it doesn't work. You might have to cut and rearrange whole chapters, get feedback that hurts your feelings, and if you try for traditional publishing, yes, you *will* get rejected a time or two.

Here's the glorious part about all of that: none of it can stop you. You can still write and publish a kick-ass book, like we said from the beginning. The power is, and has always been, in your hands. You have agency, choices, and control over your own authorial future.

There has never been a better time to write a book. The means of getting it into the hands of readers are endless and the people available to partner with you in the process are plentiful and talented. You always had the gumption; now, with this book, you have a plan. You know what creates the foundation of a solid book, how to map it all out, how to write the freaking thing, and of course, all the publishing options available to you.

So, are you gonna go for it? Are you going to share the message that's been burning a hole in your heart for so long? Are you going to join the ranks of thousands who have come before you, put pen to paper (fingers to keys), and do the thing you know you are called to do?

Write a book. Write *your* book. We sure hope you do. The world needs it. The land of authorship isn't reserved for the elite or famous or even the mega-talented. It's for anyone who has the courage to try and not give up. It's for *you*. Please write your book. Go, Hungry Author, go. Get out there and do the work. It will all be worth it. It will all work out.

Remember, you have a message and a story worth publishing—and if you've got the hunger, you can make it happen.

Acknowledgments

This book wouldn't exist without the help and encouragement of our families, colleagues, and friends.

Kent Sanders, remember when we both told you we would never, ever, ever in a million years start a podcast and we had absolutely zero interest in ever doing that? You can officially say you told us so. And thank you for suggesting that we write this book together. Apparently we get all of our best ideas from you!

Ally Fallon, our friend and mentor. Thank you for encouraging us every step of the way and for being a friend through this process. You inspire us.

Jessica Sherer, Molly Wilcox, and Ashton Renshaw, our EntreprenHER sisters, thank you for giving us feedback and listening to us kvetch every month while writing this book. We owe you one.

Merideth Hite Estevez, Ericka Andersen, Kristin Vanderlip, and Mara Eller: Thank you for reading early drafts of our proposal, chapters, and manuscript. We love you like sisters.

Amanda Bauch: Thank you for giving us such thorough feedback on our proposal. Pretty sure we got a book deal because of you!

Jeff and Chantel Goins: We've each learned so much from your mentorship. Thank you for being friends and thought partners, and for challenging us to pursue excellence in our own writing.

Christen Karniski, Joanna Wattenberg, David Bailey, and the team at Rowman & Littlefield, thank you for believing in us and gently guiding the way through the publishing process.

Don Pape, you are goodness incarnate. We can't thank you enough for advocating for us, connecting us with incredible interviewees, and supporting so many Hungry Authors.

From Liz:

Ariel, this book wouldn't exist without you. The best parts of my career wouldn't exist without you. You are the most amazing partner, writer, editor, and friend I could have asked for. You make everything shine and I'll be grateful forever you weren't weirded out by an overly familiar and enthusiastic Voxer message from a girl you hardly knew (me). Thanks for it all.

Ryan, thank you for being my most ardent supporter, cheerleader, best friend, and confidant. Every time I said I couldn't do it or wasn't good enough, you told me otherwise. I believe in myself because you've believed in me from the beginning. There aren't enough words to say how much I love you.

Weston and Fiona, anything I've ever done and will do is for you. You are my whole world. Thank you for being my reason for everything.

Mom, Dad, and Ross, thank you for being there for me my whole life. If I'm able to achieve anything at all it's because you loved me and supported me. Thank you for always loving my writing and making me feel like I can do anything.

Jack. Thank you for teaching me to not take anything too seriously and for whispering in my ear from the great beyond, during the darkest times, that we're all gonna be alright. I miss you. I love you. I wish you were here.

To my friends, Laura, Katie, Dana, Jacey, Jenny, Jenna, Meghan, and Emily, thank you for celebrating me and consistently asking about my work. Thank you for listening as I talked about this book on every walk, phone call, and dinner out. No girl has ever been as lucky as me. I adore you.

Alexis, thank you for being the best coach in the whole world and reminding me that I am talented, strong, and capable even when I didn't feel like it. You kept me going and I'm so grateful.

From Ariel:

Liz, thank you for making me laugh and cry in equal measure (and both in a good way) throughout the writing of this book. Writing is usually lonely, but for me, writing this book has been hanging out with my BFF. I feel so lucky that we get to go on this author, business, speaking, influencing adventure together. I wish every writer had a friend like you.

Arnis Burvikovs, we can trace the origin of this book back to the day at the ASCD conference when I was your editorial assistant and you told me that you thought I had what it takes to be an acquisitions editor. You gave me the greatest gift that day.

Erin Null and Tori Bachman, thank you for letting us steal the phrase "Hungry Authors" that originated at the virtual water cooler at Corwin Press. We started a movement that day, and I hope with all my heart that this book makes you proud.

Leanne and Milo, thank you for letting me live with you in London for my first internship, even though you had no idea who I was and I literally dropped on your doorstep in the middle of the night. Thanks for teaching me how to cook fish and curry. Those months with you were some of the best in my life. Your kindness so long ago set me on the path to a fulfilling career and writing this book.

Mom and Dad, thank you for being my biggest fans. Thank you for letting me pursue what probably looked like a pipedream. You've always fanned the flames of my craziest dreams. I love you so much.

Olivia and Maggie, I keep trying to be as cool as you two, and I keep failing. And then I wrote a book about writing books, so my chances are shot now.

Josh, I can't get sentimental or I'll cry. But you'll be glad to know I'm ready to start writing another book now. Thank you in advance.

Ja'Nylah and Raevynn, you will always be part of my story. What a blessing and great honor it was to mother you. I love you, I love you, I love you.

Appendix

A Writer's Reading List

We are students, and the following texts have been our mentors. The methods we have developed and explained in this book have been influenced by the ideas and advice from other, mostly more experienced authors. We're just honored to contribute whatever humble knowledge we have to the Great Conversation. If you would like to continue your journey learning about the art and logic of writing books, then we gladly point you to the following resources:

When you need inspiration:

The Writing Life by Annie Dillard
Bird by Bird: Some Instructions on Writing and Life by Anne Lamott
The War of Art: Break Through the Blocks and Win Your Inner Creative Battles by Steven Pressfield
Big Magic: Creative Living Beyond Fear by Elizabeth Gilbert
The Power of Writing It Down: A Simple Habit to Unlock Your Brain and Reimagine Your Life by Allison Fallon
You Are a Writer (So Start ACTING Like One) by Jeff Goins

When you're planning:

> *The Story Grid: What Good Editors Know* by Shawn Coyne
> *Blueprint for a Nonfiction Book: Plan and Pitch Your Big Idea*
> by Jennie Nash
> *The Art of Memoir* by Mary Karr
> *Published: The Proven Path From Blank Page to 10,000 Copies
> Sold* by Chandler Bolt
> *Big Idea to Bestseller: How to Write, Publish, and Launch a
> Nonfiction Book to Grow Your Business and Make an Impact*
> by Jake Kelfer

When you want to improve your craft:

> *Several Short Sentences About Writing* by Verlyn Klinkenborg
> *On Writing Well: The Classic Guide to Writing Nonfiction* by
> William Zinsser
> *On Writing: A Memoir of the Craft* by Stephen King

When you're ready to publish:

> *Perennial Seller: The Art of Making and Marketing Work That
> Lasts* by Ryan Holiday
> *Write Useful Books: A Modern Approach to Designing and
> Refining Recommendable Nonfiction* by Rob Fitzpatrick
> *Get Signed* by Lucinda Halpern
> *The Business of Being a Writer* by Jane Friedman
> *Before and After the Book Deal: A Writer's Guide to Finishing,
> Publishing, Promoting, and Surviving Your First Book* by
> Courtney Maum
> *How to Write a Book Proposal: The Insider's Step-by-Step
> Guide to Proposals That Get You Published*, 5th edition, by
> Jody Rein and Michael Larsen

Notes

Chapter 2

1. Shawn Coyne, *The Story Grid* (New York: Black Irish Entertainment, LLC, 2015), 56.
2. Ibid., 45.
3. William Zinsser, *On Writing Well*, seventh edition (New York: Harper Perennial, 2016), 135.

Chapter 3

1. Grant Baldwin, *The Successful Speaker* (Grand Rapids, MI: Baker Books, 2020), 46.
2. James Clear (@jamesclear), "The target audience is always the same: myself," Twitter, March 27, 2021, 9:26 p.m. https://twitter.com/JamesClear/status/1375982505531215872?lang=en.
3. Maria Popova, "Kurt Vonnegut's 8 Tenets of Storytelling," *The Marginalian*, https://www.themarginalian.org/2012/04/03/kurt-vonnegut-on-writing-stories/ (September 2023).
4. Tim Ferriss, "The Tim Ferriss Show Transcripts: The 4-Hour Workweek Revisited (#295)," *The Tim Ferriss Show*, https://tim.blog/2018/02/06/the-tim-ferriss-show-transcripts-the-4-hour-workweek-revisited/ (September 2023).

Chapter 4

1. Jennie Nash, *Blueprint for a Nonfiction Book* (Santa Barbara, CA: Tree Farm Books, 2022), 51.

Chapter 5

1. James Clear, *Atomic Habits* (New York: Penguin Random House, 2018), 9.

2. Jonathan Fields, "Jen Sincero: You Are a Badass (at Life and Money)," *The Good Life Project*, podcast, May 2017, https://www.goodlifeproject.com/podcast/jen-sincero/.

3. Jennie Nash, *Blueprint for a Nonfiction Book* (Santa Barbara, CA: Tree Farm Books, 2022), 21.

4. Ariel Curry and Liz Morrow, "Make Your Boldest Statement with Stephanie Duncan Smith," *Hungry Authors*, podcast, April 10, 2023, https://open.spotify.com/episode/5dIe8CSVsex6nVz4hopX VU?si=036907ca02784e58.

5. John Pollack, *The Pun Also Rises* (New York: Avery, 2011), 12.

6. Mike Michalowicz, *Profit First: Transform Your Business From a Cash-Eating Monster to a Money-Making Machine* (New York: Portfolio Penguin, 2017), 6.

7. Allison Fallon, *The Power of Writing It Down* (Grand Rapids, MI: Zondervan Thrive, 2021), 9.

8. Elizabeth Gilbert, *Eat, Pray, Love* (New York: Riverhead Books, 2016), xvi.

9. Susan Cain, *Bittersweet* (New York: Crown, 2022), xxii.

10. Atul Gawande, *Being Mortal* (New York: Metropolitan Books, 2014), 10.

11. Kate Bowler, *Everything Happens for a Reason* (New York: Random House, 2018), xviii.

12. Steve Tweedie, "The 14 Best Steve Jobs Quotes to Inspire Your Inner Creative Genius," *Inc.*, https://www.inc.com/business-insider/14-most-inspiring-steve-jobs-quotes.html (August 2023).

13. Courtney Tanner, "Why are these two books banned at the Utah State prison?" *Salt Lake Tribune*, https://archive.sltrib.com/article.php?id=4564871&itype=CMSID (September 2023).

14. Amazon, "Atomic Habits: An Easy & Proven Way to Build Good Habits & Break Bad Ones," product page, https://www.amazon.com/Atomic-Habits-Proven-Build-Break/dp/0735211299/ref=sr_1_1?crid=2VZ3JN40RH1TI&keywords=atomic+habits&qid=1695221595&s=books&sprefix=atomic%2Cstripbooks%2C113&sr=1-1 (August 2023).

15. Lucinda Halpern, *Get Signed* (Carlsbad, CA: Hay House, 2024), 11.

16. Eric Nelson, "The Secret to Coming Up With Ideas People Can Get Excited About," LinkedIn, https://www.linkedin.com/pulse/secret-coming-up-ideas-people-can-get-excited-eric-nelson/?trackingId=p48jrheUSLOIGebSJdXsFQ%3D%3D (Aug 2023).

17. Halpern, *Get Signed*, 12.

Chapter 6

1. Joseph Campbell, *The Hero With a Thousand Faces*, third edition (Novato, CA: New World Library, 2008), 23.

2. James Clear, *Atomic Habits* (New York: Penguin Random House, 2018), 252–53.

3. Joseph Campbell, *The Hero With a Thousand Faces*, third edition (Novato, CA: New World Library, 2008), 23.

4. Elizabeth Gilbert, *Eat, Pray, Love* (New York: Riverhead Books, 2016), 364.

Chapter 7

1. Greg McKeown, *Essentialism* (New York: Currency, 2014).

2. Stephen R. Covey, *The 7 Habits of Highly Effective People*, thirtieth anniversary edition (New York: Simon & Schuster, 2020).

3. Michael Singer, *The Surrender Experiment* (New York: Harmony Books, 2015).

4. Rachel Hollis, *Girl, Wash Your Face* (Nashville: Thomas Nelson, 2018).

5. Jen Sincero, *You Are a Badass* (Philadelphia: Running Press, 2013).

6. Donald Miller, *Marketing Made Simple* (Nashville: HarperCollins Leadership, 2020).

7. James Clear, *Atomic Habits* (New York: Penguin Random House, 2018), vii–ix.

8. Brené Brown, *Rising Strong* (New York: Spiegel & Grau, 2015), 40.

9. Glennon Doyle, *Untamed* (New York: The Dial Press, 2020).

Chapter 8

1. James Clear, *Atomic Habits* (New York: Penguin Random House, 2018), 82.

2. Peter Attia, *Outlive* (New York: Harmony Books, 2023), 145.

3. Brené Brown, *Rising Strong* (New York: Spiegel & Grau, 2015), 40.

4. Dan Pink, *To Sell Is Human* (New York: Riverhead Books, 2012), 9.

5. Ramit Sethi, *I Will Teach You to Be Rich*, second edition (New York: Workman, 2019), 188.

6. Robin Diangelo, *White Fragility* (Boston: Beacon Press, 2018), 15.

7. Verlyn Klinkenborg, *Several Short Sentences About Writing* (New York: Vintage Books, 2012), np.

8. Clear, *Atomic Habits*, 84.

9. Ibid., 85.

10. Ibid., 87.

11. Ibid., 81–83.

12. Ibid., 90.

Chapter 9

1. Leslie Watts, "Points of Connection: Story Macro and Micro," StoryGrid, https://storygrid.com/story-macro-micro/ (September 2023).

2. Elizabeth Gilbert, *Eat, Pray, Love* (New York: Riverhead Books, 2016), 9.

3. Chanel Miller, *Know My Name* (New York: Penguin Books, 2020), 52.

4. Malcolm Gladwell, *The Bomber Mafia* (New York: Little, Brown and Company, 2021), 113.

5. Amy Bloom, *In Love* (New York: Random House, 2022), 115.

6. Gilbert, *Eat, Pray, Love*, 9.

7. Ibid., 19.

Chapter 10

1. Ed Pilkington, "Malcolm Gladwell: 'I'm interested in the slightly dumb and obvious, not the deeply weird and obscure,'" *Guardian*, https://www.theguardian.com/books/2009/oct/26/malcolm-gladwell-tipping-point-blink (August 2023).

2. Dorie Clark, "How to Promote Yourself Without Looking Like a Jerk," *Harvard Business Review*, https://hbr.org/2014/12/how-to-promote-yourself-without-looking-like-a-jerk (August 2023).

3. Lawrence R. Samuel, "Why Do Writers Write?" *Psychology Today*, https://www.psychologytoday.com/us/blog/psychology-yesterday/201802/why-do-writers-write (September 2023).

4. Table 4. Quits levels and rates by industry and region, seasonally adjusted—2023 M09 Results, https://www.bls.gov/news.release/jolts.nr0.htm.

5. *You've Got Mail*, directed by Nora Ephron (New York: Warner Home Video, 1998).

6. Annie Dillard, *The Writing Life* (New York: HarperCollins Publishers, 1989), 78.

Chapter 11

1. Steven Pressfield, *The War of Art* (New York: Black Irish Entertainment, LLC, 2002), 74.

2. Rob Fitzgerald, *Write Useful Books* ([No location]: Useful Books Ltd., 2021), 55.

3. Annie Dillard, *The Writing Life* (New York: HarperCollins Publishers, 1989), 15.

Chapter 12

1. Mason Currey, *Daily Rituals* (New York: Alfred A. Knopf, 2013), 52, 53, 176.

2. Cheryl Strayed, "Dear Sugar, The Rumpus Advice Column #48: Write Like a Motherfucker," *The Rumpus*, https://therumpus. net/2010/08/19/dear-sugar-the-rumpus-advice-column-48-write -like-a-motherfucker/ (September 2023).

3. Benjamin Hardy, "This Morning Routine Will Make You Unstoppable," *Thrive Global*, https://medium.com/thrive-global/ this-morning-routine-will-make-you-a-millionaire-f2309d8005aa (September 2023).

4. Julia Cameron, *The Artist's Way: A Spiritual Path to Higher Creativity*, twenty-fifth anniversary edition (New York: TarcherPerigee, 2016), 16.

5. B. J. Shannon, et al., "Morning-Evening Variation in Human B rain Metabolism and Memory Circuits," *Journal of Neurophysiology* 109, no. 5 (2013): 1444–56, https://doi.org/10.1152/jn.00651.2012.

6. Brené Brown, *Rising Strong* (New York: Spiegel & Grau, 2015), 12.

7. Gretchen Reynolds, "Can Exercise Make You More Creative?" *New York Times*, https://www.nytimes.com/2021/02/03/well/ exercise-creativity.html (August 2023).

8. Lorenza Colzato, et al., "The Impact of Physical Exercise on Convergent and Divergent Thinking," *Frontiers in Human Neuroscience* 7 (2013), https://doi.org/10.3389/fnhum.2013.00824.

9. Rachel Held Evans, Rachel Held Evans Legacy Facebook post, https://www.facebook.com/rachelheldevans.page/photos/just -for-fun-heres-a-picture-of-the-mantrainspiration-board-above-my -writing-des/10154276896214442/ (October 10, 2016).

10. Ron Friedman, "Your Brain's Ideal Schedule." *Harvard Business Review IdeaCast*, March 26, 2015, podcast, 23:42. https://hbr. org/podcast/2015/03/your-brains-ideal-schedule.html.

Chapter 13

1. Ryan Holiday, "Garland Robinette On the Stoic Principle That Shapes His Incredible Life," *The Daily Stoic*, July 1, 2023, podcast, 01:26:57. https://open.spotify.com/episode/27hvyA7oAGGxDHb c5CuInx?si=cccbd8a27e854e78.

2. Ryan Holiday, *Perennial Seller* (New York: Portfolio, 2017), 76.

3. Sir Arthur Quiller-Crouch, "XII. On Style," *On the Art of Writing* (Cambridge: University Press, 1916), https://www.bartleby.com/lit-hub/on-the-art-of-writing/.

4. Heather Wolpert-Gawron, *Just Ask Us* (Thousand Oaks, CA: Corwin, 2018), 5.

5. Rachelle Gardner, "What Is Writer's Voice?" Gardner Literary, https://rachellegardner.com/what-is-writers-voice/ (August 2023).

Chapter 14

1. James N. Green and Peter Stallybrass, "Section 6: Inventing Poor Richard," The Library Company of Philadelphia, Exhibition, 2006, https://www.librarycompany.org/BFWriter/poor.htm (September 2023).

2. Joseph Viscomi, "Archive Exhibition: Illuminated Printing by Joseph Viscomi (April 2019)," The William Blake Archive, https://www.blakearchive.org/exhibit/illuminatedprinting (September 2023).

3. The Jane Austen Society of North America, "*Sense and Sensibility*," https://jasna.org/austen/works/sense-sensibility/ (September 2023).

4. Kate Moore, *The Woman They Could Not Silence* (Naperville, IL: Sourcebooks, 2021), 353–59.

5. *Britannica*, "Samizdat: Soviet literature," https://www.britannica.com/technology/samizdat (September 2023).

6. Sonam Joshi, "Everyone said the literary world would laugh at me but I didn't care: Rupi Kaur," *Times of India*, https://timesofindia.indiatimes.com/home/sunday-times/everyone-said-the-literary-world-would-laugh-at-me-but-i-didnt-care-rupi-kaur/articleshow/79698748.cms (September 2023).

Chapter 15

1. Elizabeth A. Harris, Alexandra Alter, and Adam Bednar, "A Trial Put Publishing's Inner Workings on Display. What Did We Learn?" *New York Times*, https://www.nytimes.com/2022/08/19/books/prh-penguin-random-house-trial.html (August 2023).

2. Joel J. Miller, "Bookish Diversions: Publishing Boom and Bust," *Miller's Book Review*, https://www.millersbookreview.com/p/publishing-boom-and-bust?r=1jgly3&utm_campaign=post&utm_medium=email (August 2023).

3. Dean Talbot, "Book Publishing Companies Statistics," WordsRated, https://wordsrated.com/book-publishing-companies-statistics/#:~:text=The%20Big%20Five%20publishers&text=Over%2080%25%20of%20the%20US,the%20US%20publishing%20industry's%20revenue (September 2023).

4. Catherine Baab-Muguira, "You Don't Need a Platform If You Can Find an Audience," Janefriedman.com, https://janefriedman.com/you-dont-need-a-platform-if-you-can-find-an-audience/ (August 2023).

5. Elizabeth A. Harris, "Millions of Followers? For Book Sales, 'It's Unreliable,'" *The New York Times*, https://www.nytimes.com/2021/12/07/books/social-media-following-book-publishing.html?referringSource=articleShare (August 2023).

Chapter 17

1. Independent Book Publishers Association, "Independent Book Publishers Association's (IBPA's) Hybrid Publisher Criteria," https://www.ibpa-online.org/resource/resmgr/docs/IBPA-Hybrid-Publisher-Criter.pdf (August 2023).

Bibliography

Amazon. "Atomic Habits: An Easy & Proven Way to Build Good Habits & Break Bad Ones." Product page. https://www.amazon.com/Atomic-Habits-Proven-Build-Break/dp/0735211299/ref=sr_1_1?crid=2VZ3JN40RH1TI&keywords=atomic+habits&qid=1695221595&s=books&sprefix=atomic%2Cstripbooks%2C113&sr=1-1.

Attia, Peter. *Outlive: The Science & Art of Longevity.* New York: Harmony Books, 2023.

Baab-Muguira, Catherine. "You Don't Need a Platform If You Can Find an Audience." Janefriedman.com. Last modified November 16, 2022. Accessed August 25, 2023. https://janefriedman.com/you-dont-need-a-platform-if-you-can-find-an-audience/.

Baldwin, Grant. *The Successful Speaker: Five Steps for Booking Gigs, Getting Paid, and Building Your Platform.* Grand Rapids, MI: Baker Books, 2020.

Beahm, George, ed. *I, Steve: Steve Jobs in His Own Words.* Evanston, IL: Agate Publishing Inc., 2011.

Bloom, Amy. *In Love: A Memoir of Love and Loss.* New York: Random House, 2022.

Bowler, Kate. *Everything Happens for a Reason: And Other Lies I've Loved.* New York: Random House, 2018.

Britannica. "Samizdat: Soviet literature." Last modified December 31, 2014. Accessed September 2023. https://www.britannica.com/technology/samizdat.

Brown, Brené. *Rising Strong: The Reckoning, The Rumble, The Revolution.* New York: Spiegel & Grau, 2015.

Cain, Susan. *Bittersweet: How Sorrow and Longing Make Us Whole.* New York: Crown, 2022.

Cameron, Julia. *The Artist's Way: A Spiritual Path to Higher Creativity.* twenty-fifth anniversary edition. New York: TarcherPerigee, 2016.

Campbell, Joseph. *The Hero With a Thousand Faces.* Third edition. Novato, CA: New World Library, 2008.

Clark, Dorie. "How to Promote Yourself Without Looking Like a Jerk." *Harvard Business Review.* Last modified December 22, 2014. Accessed September 2023. https://hbr.org/2014/12/how-to-promote-yourself-without-looking-like-a-jerk.

Clear, James. *Atomic Habits: An Easy & Proven Way to Build Good Habits & Break Bad Ones.* New York: Penguin Random House, 2018.

Clear, James (@jamesclear). "The target audience is always the same: myself." Twitter, March 27, 2021, 9:26 p.m. https://twitter.com/JamesClear/status/1375982505531215872?lang=en.

Colzato, Lorenza S., Ayca Szapora, Justine N. Pannekoek, and Bernhard Hommel. "The Impact of Physical Exercise on Convergent and Divergent Thinking." *Frontiers in Human Neuroscience* 7 (December 2013). https://doi.org/10.3389/fnhum.2013.00824.

Covey, Stephen R. *The 7 Habits of Highly Effective People*, thirtieth anniversary edition. New York: Simon & Schuster, 2020.

Coyne, Shawn. *The Story Grid: What Editors Know.* New York: Black Irish Entertainment, LLC, 2015.

Currey, Mason. *Daily Rituals: How Artists Work.* New York: Alfred A. Knopf, 2013.

Curry, Ariel, and Liz Morrow. "Make Your Boldest Statement with Stephanie Duncan Smith." *Hungry Authors,* April 10, 2023, Podcast, 00:47:55. https://open.spotify.com/episode/5dIe8CSVsex6nVz4hopXVU?si=036907ca02784e58.

Diangelo, Robin. *White Fragility: Why It's So Hard for White People to Talk About Racism.* Boston: Beacon Press, 2018.

Dillard, Annie. *The Writing Life.* New York: HarperCollins Publishers, 1989.

Doyle, Glennon. *Untamed.* New York: The Dial Press, 2020.

Ephron, Nora, dir. *You've Got Mail*. New York: Warner Home Video, 1998.

Fallon, Allison. *The Power of Writing It Down*. Grand Rapids, MI: Zondervan Thrive, 2021.

Ferriss, Tim. "*The Tim Ferriss Show* Transcripts: The 4-Hour Workweek Revisited (#295)." *The Tim Ferriss Show*. Last modified February 6, 2018. Accessed September 2023. https://tim .blog/2018/02/06/the-tim-ferriss-show-transcripts-the-4-hour -workweek-revisited/.

Fields, Jonathan. "Jen Sincero: You Are a Badass (at Life and Money)," *The Good Life Project*, May 2017, Podcast, 54:45. https:// www.goodlifeproject.com/podcast/jen-sincero/.

Fitzgerald, Rob. *Write Useful Books: A Modern Approach to Designing and Refining Recommendable Nonfiction*. [No location]: Useful Books Ltd., 2021.

Friedman, Jane. "IMHO: How Much Does Platform Matter?" *The Hot Sheet*. Accessed January 2023. https://hotsheetpub.com/ 2022/07/imho-how-much-does-platform-matter/.

Friedman, Ron. "Your Brain's Ideal Schedule." *Harvard Business Review IdeaCast*, March 26, 2015, Podcast, 23:42. https://hbr.org/ podcast/2015/03/your-brains-ideal-schedule.html.

Gardner, Rachelle. "What Is Writer's Voice?" Gardner Literary. Last modified July 30, 2010. Accessed August 2023. https://rachelle gardner.com/what-is-writers-voice/.

Gawande, Atul. *Being Mortal: Medicine and What Matters in the End*. New York: Metropolitan Books, 2014.

Gilbert, Elizabeth. *Eat, Pray, Love*. New York: Riverhead Books, 2016.

Gladwell, Malcolm. *The Bomber Mafia: A Dream, a Temptation, and the Longest Night of the Second World War*. New York: Little, Brown and Company, 2021.

Green, James N., and Peter Stallybrass. "Section 6: Inventing Poor Richard." The Library Company of Philadelphia, Exhibition, 2006. Accessed September 2023. https://www.librarycompany.org/ BFWriter/poor.htm.

Halpern, Lucinda. *Get Signed*. Carlsbad, CA: Hay House, 2024.

Hardy, Benjamin. "This Morning Routine Will Make You Unstoppable." *Thrive Global*. Last modified August 24, 2018. Accessed September 2023. https://medium.com/thrive-global/this -morning-routine-will-make-you-a-millionaire-f2309d8005aa.

Harris, Elizabeth A. "Millions of Followers? For Book Sales, 'It's Unreliable.'" *New York Times*. Last modified December 21, 2021. Accessed August 25, 2023. https://www.nytimes.com/2021/12/07/books/social-media-following-book-publishing.html?referringSource=articleShare.

Harris, Elizabeth A., Alexandra Alter, and Adam Bednar. "A Trial Put Publishing's Inner Workings on Display. What Did We Learn?" *New York Times*. Last modified August 19, 2022. Accessed August 25, 2023. https://www.nytimes.com/2022/08/19/books/prh-penguin-random-house-trial.html.

Holiday, Ryan. "Garland Robinette On the Stoic Principle That Shapes His Incredible Life." *The Daily Stoic*, July 1, 2023. Podcast, 01:26:57. https://open.spotify.com/episode/27hvyA7oAGGxDHbc5CuInx?si=cccbd8a27e854e78.

———. *Perennial Seller: The Art of Making and Marketing Work That Lasts*. New York: Portfolio/Penguin, 2017.

Hollis, Rachel. *Girl, Wash Your Face: Stop Believing the Lies About Who You Are So You Can Become Who You Were Meant to Be*. Nashville: Thomas Nelson, 2018.

Independent Book Publishers Association. "Independent Book Publishers Association's (IBPA's) Hybrid Publisher Criteria." Last modified September 1, 2022. Accessed August 29, 2023. https://www.ibpa-online.org/resource/resmgr/docs/IBPA-Hybrid-Publisher-Criter.pdf.

Jane Austen Society of North America, The. "*Sense and Sensibility*." [No date]. Accessed September 2023. https://jasna.org/austen/works/sense-sensibility/.

Joshi, Sonam. "Everyone said the literary world would laugh at me but I didn't care: Rupi Kaur." *Times of India*. Last modified December 13, 2020. Accessed September 2023. https://timesofindia.indiatimes.com/home/sunday-times/everyone-said-the-literary-world-would-laugh-at-me-but-i-didnt-care-rupi-kaur/articleshow/79698748.cms.

Klinkenborg, Verlyn. *Several Short Sentences About Writing*. New York: Vintage Books, 2012.

McKeown, Greg. *Essentialism: The Disciplined Pursuit of Less*. New York: Currency, 2014.

Michalowicz, Mike. *Profit First: Transform Your Business From a Cash-Eating Monster to a Money-Making Machine*. New York: Portfolio Penguin, 2017.

Miller, Chanel. *Know My Name: A Memoir*. New York: Penguin Books, 2020.

Miller, Donald. *Marketing Made Simple: A Step-by-Step StoryBrand Guide for Any Business*. Nashville: HarperCollins Leadership, 2020.

Miller, Joel J. "Bookish Diversions: Publishing Boom and Bust." *Miller's Book Review*. Last modified August 2, 2023. Accessed August 2, 2023. https://www.millersbookreview.com/p/publishing-boom-and-bust?r=1jgly3&utm_campaign=post&utm_medium=email.

Moore, Kate. *The Woman They Could Not Silence*. Naperville, IL: Sourcebooks, 2021.

Nash, Jennie. *Blueprint for a Nonfiction Book: Plan and Pitch Your Big Idea*. Santa Barbara, CA: Tree Farm Books, 2022.

Nelson, Eric. "The Secret to Coming Up With Ideas People Can Get Excited About." LinkedIn. Last modified September 19, 2017. Accessed August 2023. https://www.linkedin.com/pulse/secret-coming-up-ideas-people-can-get-excited-eric-nelson/?trackingId=p48jrheUSLOIGebSJdXsFQ%3D%3D.

Pilkington, Ed. "Malcolm Gladwell: 'I'm interested in the slightly dumb and obvious, not the deeply weird and obscure.'" *Guardian*. Last modified October 25, 2009. Accessed August 2023. https://www.theguardian.com/books/2009/oct/26/malcolm-gladwell-tipping-point-blink.

Pink, Daniel. *To Sell Is Human: The Surprising Truth About Moving Others*. New York: Riverhead Books, 2012.

Pollack, John. *The Pun Also Rises: How the Humble Pun Revolutionized Language, Changed History, and Made Wordplay More Than Some Antics*. New York: Avery, 2011.

Popova, Maria. "Kurt Vonnegut's 8 Tenets of Storytelling." *The Marginalian*. [No date]. Accessed September 2023. https://www.themarginalian.org/2012/04/03/kurt-vonnegut-on-writing-stories/.

Pressfield, Steven. *The War of Art: Break Through the Blocks and Win Your Inner Creative Battles*. New York: Black Irish Entertainment, LLC, 2002.

Quiller-Crouch, Sir Arthur. "XII. On Style." *On the Art of Writing.* Cambridge: University Press, 1916. https://www.bartleby.com/lit-hub/on-the-art-of-writing/.

Reynolds, Gretchen. "Can Exercise Make You More Creative?" *New York Times.* Last modified February 5, 2021. Accessed August 2023. https://www.nytimes.com/2021/02/03/well/exercise-creativity.html.

Samuel, Lawrence R. "Why Do Writers Write?" *Psychology Today.* Last modified February 14, 2018. Accessed September 2023. https://www.psychologytoday.com/us/blog/psychology-yesterday/201802/why-do-writers-write.

Sanders, Kent. "Publishing Panel." Conference Session. Refined Conference, Market Refined Media, September 16, 2023.

Sethi, Ramit. *I Will Teach You to Be Rich: No Guilt. No Excuses. No BS. Just a 6-Week Program That Works.* Second edition. New York: Workman Publishing, 2019.

Shannon, B. J., R. A. Dosenbach, Y. Su, A. G. Vlassenko, L. J. Larson-Prior, T. S. Nolan, A. Z. Snyder, and M. E. Raichle. "Morning-Evening Variation in Human Brain Metabolism and Memory Circuits." *Journal of Neurophysiology* 109, no. 5 (March 2013): 1444–56. https://doi.org/10.1152/jn.00651.2012.

Sincero, Jen. *You Are a Badass: How to Stop Doubting Your Greatness and Start Living an Awesome Life.* Philadelphia: Running Press, 2013.

Singer, Michael. *The Surrender Experiment: My Journey into Life's Perfection.* New York: Harmony Books, 2015.

Strayed, Cheryl. "Dear Sugar, The Rumpus Advice Column #48: Write Like a Motherfucker." *The Rumpus.* Last modified August 19, 2010. Accessed September 2023. https://therumpus.net/2010/08/19/dear-sugar-the-rumpus-advice-column-48-write-like-a-motherfucker/.

———. *Wild: From Lost to Found on the Pacific Crest Trail.* New York: Vintage Books, 2012.

Talbot, Dean. "Book Publishing Companies Statistics." WordsRated. Last modified January 27, 2023. Accessed September 2023. https://wordsrated.com/book-publishing-companies-statistics/#:~:text=The%20Big%20Five%20publishers&text=Over%2080%25%20of%20the%20US,the%20US%20publishing%20industry's%20revenue.

Tanner, Courtney. "Why are these two books banned at the Utah State prison?" *Salt Lake Tribune*. Last modified January 9, 2017. Accessed September 2023. https://archive.sltrib.com/article.php?id=4564871&itype=CMSID.

Tweedie, Steve. "The 14 Best Steve Jobs Quotes to Inspire Your Inner Creative Genius." *Inc*. Last modified July 13, 2015. Accessed August 2023. https://www.inc.com/business-insider/14-most-inspiring-steve-jobs-quotes.html.

Viscomi, Joseph. The William Blake Archive. "Archive Exhibition: Illuminated Printing by Joseph Viscomi (April 2019)." Accessed September 2023. https://www.blakearchive.org/exhibit/illuminatedprinting.

Watts, Leslie. "Points of Connection: Story Macro and Micro." StoryGrid. [No date]. Accessed September 2023. https://storygrid.com/story-macro-micro/.

Wolpert-Gawron, Heather. *Just Ask Us: Kids Speak Out on Student Engagement*. Thousand Oaks, CA: Corwin, 2018.

Zinsser, William. *On Writing Well: The Classic Guide to Writing Nonfiction*. Seventh edition. New York: Harper Perennial, 2016.

Index

Page numbers in italics refer to figures and tables.

About the Authors

Liz Morrow is a traditionally published ghostwriter for entrepreneurs, thought leaders, and business experts. She specializes in personal and professional development and memoir. Though she has experience in every piece of the pipeline—including book ideation, planning, positioning, editing, and marketing—writing has always been the part she loves most. She is proud to have worked with authors such as Grant Baldwin, Jeff Goins, Pat Flynn, and Whitney English and publishers such as Baker Books, Harper Horizon, Harper Leadership, and Hay House.

When she's not writing, you can find Liz listening to long-form podcasts, rewatching *The Office*, and drinking margaritas with friends. She lives in Greenville, South Carolina, with her husband, two children, and goldendoodle.

Ariel Curry is a ghostwriter, editor, and book coach at Ariel Curry Editorial with over ten years of experience in traditional publishing. For seven of those years, she managed three multimillion-dollar publishing lists, acquiring leadership, teaching, and technology books. She now specializes in developing prescriptive nonfiction and memoirs. As an editor, she enjoys brainstorming and outlining new book ideas, bringing clarity and purpose to prose, and helping authors build their self-efficacy. She has collaborated with authors such as Jeff Goins, TED speaker Sugata Mitra, *New York Times* columnist Warren Berger, supermodel Genevieve Morton, and TV producer Matt Williams.

When she's not working on books, you can find Ariel doing yoga, playing piano, beekeeping, or reading with a glass of wine. She lives in Chattanooga, Tennessee, with her husband, foster children, and their rescue dogs, Enyo and Tenaya.